HEATH ROBINSON
CONTRAPTIONS

"The Aeronaut", an illustration for *The Adventures of Uncle Lubin* published by Grant Richards in 1902. It was in this book that Heath Robinson's contraptions first appeared. This and a number of the other original illustrations, although originally published in black and white, were subsequently coloured for exhibition.

HEATH ROBINSON
CONTRAPTIONS

Edited by Geoffrey Beare

DUCKWORTH

This edition published in 2021 by Duckworth,
an imprint of Duckworth Books Ltd,
1 Golden Court, Richmond, TW9 1EU, United Kingdom
www.duckworthbooks.co.uk

First published in 2007 by Duckworth Overlook

Copyright © 2007 The Estate of Mrs J.C. Robinson
Text copyright © 2007 by Geoffrey Beare

All rights reserved. No part of this publication
may be reproduced, stored in a retrieval system, or
transmitted, in any form or by any means, electronic,
mechanical, photocopying, recording or otherwise,
without the prior permission of the publisher.

A catalogue record for this book is available
from the British Library

ISBN 9781788423816

Printed and bound in the UK by
Bell and Bain Ltd, Glasgow

William Heath Robinson pictured in his studio in about 1936.

INTRODUCTION

WILLIAM HEATH ROBINSON (seen here at work in the mid-1930s) was born in Islington in May, 1872. His formal training as an artist began at a small art school in North London and was continued at the Royal Academy Schools. On graduating his first inclination was to landscape painting, which remained his first love throughout his life, but economic realities soon forced him to turn to a more readily saleable form of art. His older brothers Charles and Tom had already established themselves as book illustrators, and he joined them, starting in a small room off his father's studio. Although his first attempts to secure work met with little success, he eventually gained commissions for magazine illustrations, his first published drawings appearing in *The Sunday Magazine*, illustrating a serial called "The Story of Hannah" by WJ Dawson.

His first commissions for book illustrations came in 1897 from Bliss, Sands & Co. who claimed to publish "The cheapest books in the world". They specialised in the school and Sunday school prize markets and the titles included *Don Quixote, Pilgrim's Progress* and a collection of Andersen's fairy tales. By 1900 he had established himself as one of the country's leading illustrators with a wonderful set of decorative line drawings for an edition of the *Poems of Edgar Alan Poe* in which he embraced the *art nouveau style*.

But it was not until 1902 that he attained a degree of financial security, with the publication by Grant Richards of *The Adventures of Uncle Lubin*, a children's book that he wrote as well as illustrated. In it we see Heath Robinson's sense of humour coming to the fore, together with early examples of his gadgets. In his autobiography he said that Uncle Lubin had led him into new paths. Among other things, the book led to a commission to produce drawings for advertisements for a company called the Lamson Paragon Supply Company.

"Haunted by a strange little genius", an illustration for *My Line of Life*, Blackie & Son, 1938.

For Grant Richards he went on to illustrate an edition of tales from the Arabian Nights adapted for very young children, before taking on a commission that was totally different in nature and scale. This was to illustrate *The Works of Rabelais* with 100 full-page and well over 100 smaller headpieces and vignettes. It was to appear in two fat quarto volumes bound in white buckram and decorated in gilt. The costs involved in printing this extravagant edition contributed to the failure of the publishing house of Grant Richards, which was announced in November 1904. After protracted negotiations the creditors, of whom Heath Robinson was one, were paid 2/- in the pound.

Heath Robinson started to look for new sources of income, especially for commissions that would yield immediate payment. His best prospect lay with the quality weekly magazines which featured a number of full-page humorous drawings in each issue. In his first humorous drawings he set out to satirise the late-Victorian and Edwardian taste for allegorical paintings on themes such as "Love" or "Hope". He did not find them easy to sell. In his autobiography he recalls that one editor, having looked through his portfolio, remarked: "If this work is humorous, your serious work must be very serious indeed." He persuaded *The Tatler* to accept some of them and between March 1905 and February 1906 they published a total of eighteen drawings.

However, he soon hit his stride. In an article entitled 'The Delicacy of Humour' published in *The Ladies' Realm* in December 1907, Marion Hepworth Dixon said that:

> Mr W. Heath Robinson is an artist at once so thorough, so conscientious and so original that he can be compared for the moment only with himself. A quaint exaggeration may be said to be the source of his humour, a humour that, unlike that of most of his contemporaries, needs little illumination or explanation in the way of accompanying text.

Later in the same article she draws the reader's attention to what she describes as "the really poetic" landscapes in many of his comic pictures. It is ironic that it should have been in his humorous pictures that Heath Robinson found his first real opportunity to display his talents as a landscape artist, for in many of them the most absurd activities take place in beautifully realised settings. He seems to have been fascinated by light reflected on water, and his favourite backgrounds are the flat wet countryside of East Anglia, the seaside or the sea itself, each of which he captures in a combination of pen, pencil and watercolour.

By 1912 Heath Robinson was widely known for his contraptions, and *The Illustrated London News* reviewing his new children's book, *Bill the Minder*, introduced him as:

> . . . the fantastic limner of the dust-heap, the lumber room, the battered tin can, the strange bird and the stranger inhuman being, which contribute the material of his queer makeshift mechanical devices.

The essence of Heath Robinson's humour lies not in his strange machinery, but in his observation of ordinary people, especially those who take themselves too seriously. The contraptions were just one way of illustrating the absurd lengths to which they would go to achieve the most trivial of ends. He set out to deflate the pompous or the pretentious by exaggerating their folly to the point of absurdity, and it was not only individuals that were the butt of his humour, for he was equally likely to apply his pen to organizations and institutions, the laws of physics or the workings of fate.

In many ways, Heath Robinson's humour is seen at its best in the drawings that he made before the First World War. At that time he was approaching his peak as a serious illustrator and this is reflected in the high technical quality of the pictures. He was also free of the constraints imposed by the expectations of art editors who were later to develop a very precise notion of what a Heath Robinson cartoon should look like, and so we see a number of bold experiments in both subject matter and treatment. In some of the pictures there is wild surrealism combined with a streak of the macabre that was later subdued, either by the artist himself, or by editors unwilling to take risks with the sensibilities of their readers.

His work was popular not only in Britain, but also in Europe and the America, his drawings for *The Sketch* being syndicated to magazines in France, Germany and the USA. He was also commissioned to make drawings especially for American magazines. The example below, made in 1913 for *Harpers Bazaar* magazine, illustrated an article called "American Peril" on the activities of Americans abroad, and shows souvenir hunters at the parish church.

Although Heath Robinson's career as an illustrator continued beyond 1914, the onset of the war had spelled the end of the deluxe gift book. He wrote that even in the autumn of 1914:

> Publishers were beginning to restrict their enterprise within narrower channels, and these were all connected with the war. There was now no demand for purely artistic productions, for new editions of Shakespeare or other classics, unless they bore some connections with the all-absorbing topic.

However, if the onset of war reduced his employment as illustrator, it greatly increased the demand for his comic drawings. As early as 1909 he had drawn a series of cartoons for *The Sketch* called 'Am Tag' prompted by current reports that a German invasion was imminent. The first six drawings showed various ways in which the German army might try to enter Britain covertly, whilst the remainder show how the Territorial Army, by various subterfuges and inventions, would overcome the invading force. When the war really started in 1914, Heath Robinson had already demonstrated his ability to counter, by the application of gentle satire and absurdity, both the pompous German propaganda and the fear and depression engendered by the horrors of war. What better antidote to the stories of 'baby-eating Huns' than Heath Robinson's drawing of "The Hun" using not mustard gas, but laughing gas to disable British troops. Heath Robinson's wartime cartoons for magazines were extremely popular with both servicemen and civilians. They were collected in books such as *Some Frightful War Pictures*, published by Duckworth in 1915, followed a year later by a similar collection called *Hunlikely*.

Obvious subjects for the 'Heath Robinson' treatment were the early aeroplanes and airships, and in the later years of the war, *Flying* magazine commissioned a series of cartoons. These pictures gave the artist the ideal opportunity to combine his mechanical contraptions with his wartime satires. They also gave him a chance to draw landscape from an elevated viewpoint, showing small figures in foreshortened perspective, looking up in amazement, which he often used to good effect in succeeding years.

Once the flow of commissions for book illustration had dried up after WWI, Heath Robinson had to fall back on advertising work and humorous drawings for magazines to earn his living. During the 1920s he was contributing a weekly cartoon to *The Bystander* magazine and he was also a regular contributor to a number of other periodicals. While the majority of Heath Robinson's drawings for *The Bystander* were in black and white, in the weekly drawing for special numbers at such times as Easter, Summer or Christmas, he was allowed a second colour. He seemed to take extra care with these drawings. The characters take their ridiculous activities so seriously that the viewer is forced to hesitate and ask whether the idea is so silly after all. This is reinforced by the quality of execution. Heath Robinson acknowledged that in order for his humorous drawings to achieve their effect, the viewer had to be convinced that the artist took the activities depicted as seriously as the protagonists themselves. The primary subject matter for Heath Robinson's humorous work was not gadgets and contraptions, but the human condition, the workings of fate and the weakness and self-importance of man. This is clearly illustrated in his drawing "Testing artificial teeth in a modern tooth works". At first sight this appears to be just another 'gadget' drawing, albeit a particularly magnificent one, but like many of his drawings it has a deeper significance. The massive size of the machine compared with the objects to be tested and the large number of technicians and managers diligently pursuing their appointed tasks all serve to satirise the pomposity, fussiness and self-importance of the 'experts'. The effect is only heightened by the quality of the painting and the fine industrial landscape that provides the backdrop to the proceedings.

The Second World War saddened Heath Robinson, filling him with a sense of weariness and futility and he referred to it as 'this disastrous war'. As in the previous conflict, his humorous drawings were much in demand, and he was given a page in *The Sketch* each week. He invented the 'sixth column', a band of civilians whose aim was to frustrate the evil plans of the fifth column and made a series of pictures chronicling their exploits. The most spectacular of them shows the dislodging of a machine gun nest in the dome of St Paul's cathedral. During the First World War it was the enemy soldiers and their behaviour that provided the majority of the subjects for his cartoons. This time most of the jokes feature British soldiers or even civilians coping on the home front, and one feels that the Nazi enemy was too terrible to be the subject of such a gentle humorist.

Heath Robinson died on 13th September 1944. The portrait of Heath Robinson at the start of this introduction shows him at work in his studio in about 1936. It is significant that he chooses to be photographed with examples of his watercolours, magazine cover designs and illustrations, but there is not a humorous drawing in sight. His immediate appeal and general popularity during his lifetime resulted mainly from his humorous work and in this field he was both brilliant and unique. He was an unusually prolific artist with a seemingly inexhaustible stock of good ideas. But like artists such as Hogarth and Rowlandson before him, the secret of his appeal lay in his great abilities as a serious artist.

Geoffrey Beare

GREAT BRITISH INDUSTRY – DULY PROTECTED

Kippering Herrings by the side of the River Yare.

GREAT BRITISH INDUSTRY – DULY PROTECTED

Ox-tailing Soup.

GREAT BRITISH INDUSTRY – DULY PROTECTED

Stiltonising Cheese in the Stockyards of Cheddar.

GREAT BRITISH INDUSTRY – DULY PROTECTED

In the Pea-Splitting Sheds of a Soup Factory.

GREAT BRITISH INDUSTRY – DULY PROTECTED

The Halfpenny Testing Department of the Mint.

GREAT BRITISH INDUSTRY – DULY PROTECTED

Brewing Anchovy Sauce.

GREAT BRITISH INDUSTRY – DULY PROTECTED

In the Pressing Rooms of a Lemonade distillery.

GREAT BRITISH INDUSTRY – DULY PROTECTED

Testing Artificial Teeth in a Dental Laboratory.

Testing Gold with Uncle at the Mint.

Analysing H²0 at the Metropolitan Water Board.

CHRISTMAS PREPARATIONS – IN HEATH ROBINSONLAND

Testing the Efficacy of Mistletoe Destined for the London Market.

CHRISTMAS PREPARATIONS – IN HEATH ROBINSONLAND

Training the Young Wait.

CHRISTMAS PREPARATIONS – IN HEATH ROBINSONLAND

Luring Turkeys for Christmas Consumption.

CHRISTMAS PREPARATIONS – IN HEATH ROBINSONLAND

Testing the Plum Puddings.

The Solemn Investiture and Swearing-in of a New Boy.

Hair-Cutting Day.

Medicine Morning.

Why go as far as Epsom to see Racing? Heath Robinson's Device for Bringing the "Blue Ribbon" to your Door.
(It is clear that Mr Heath Robinson has been inspired by the spirited and realistic chariot-racing in "Ben-Hur"; and perhaps by those cycle-racing machines which are to be seen at exhibitions.).

The Editing and production of The Sketch – In the Editorial Department: the Editor and some of his Staff at Work.

This was Prepared for August! How to Keep Cool in the Hot Weather.

"THE SKETCH" CINEMA CO.! FILM-MAKING SECRETS

Making the motor dashing towards you effect: Creating the Pictures for "Horse-Power Versus Horse; or, the Car that Could not be Caught".

The steam-roller running over the bishop; Making the Pictures for "Saved by his Apron".

"THE SKETCH" CINEMA CO.! FILM-MAKING SECRETS

The cowboy pursued in the Rockies by policemen, about to Plunge into the Roaring Cataract: Making the Pictures for "Thrice-hanged Harry: the Terror of the Gulch".

"THE SKETCH" CINEMA CO.! FILM-MAKING SECRETS

Working the run-away express – for "The Girl who Slipped at the Siding".

"THE SKETCH" CINEMA CO.! FILM-MAKING SECRETS

For the European Holiday Series – Making the "Sunset on the Adriatic" pictures.

A Great but Defeated Army: "The Turks evacuating Scutari".

WORLD WAR I

German Breaches of the Hague Convention – Huns using siphons of laughing gas
to overcome our troops before an attack in close formation.

The Pilsner Pump for stealing the enemy's supper beer.

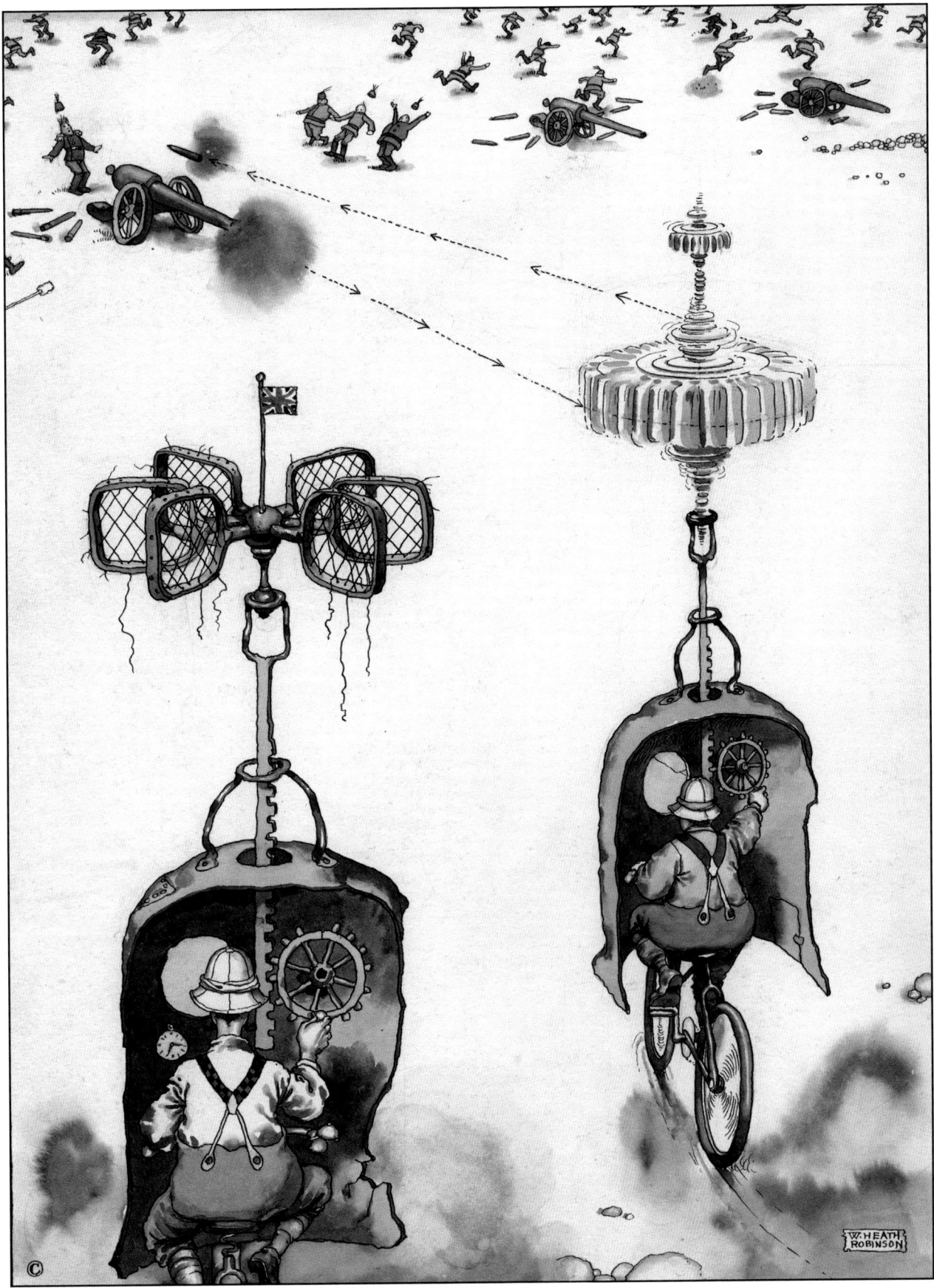

The Gallipoli shell diverter for returning the enemy's fire.

A useful attachment carried by gas bags for dental purposes.

American barb-trousers.

High art as a sauce to a low diet.

The winkle squirt.

Pre-Concerted measures against a threatened housemaid strike. Sensible provision by the government.

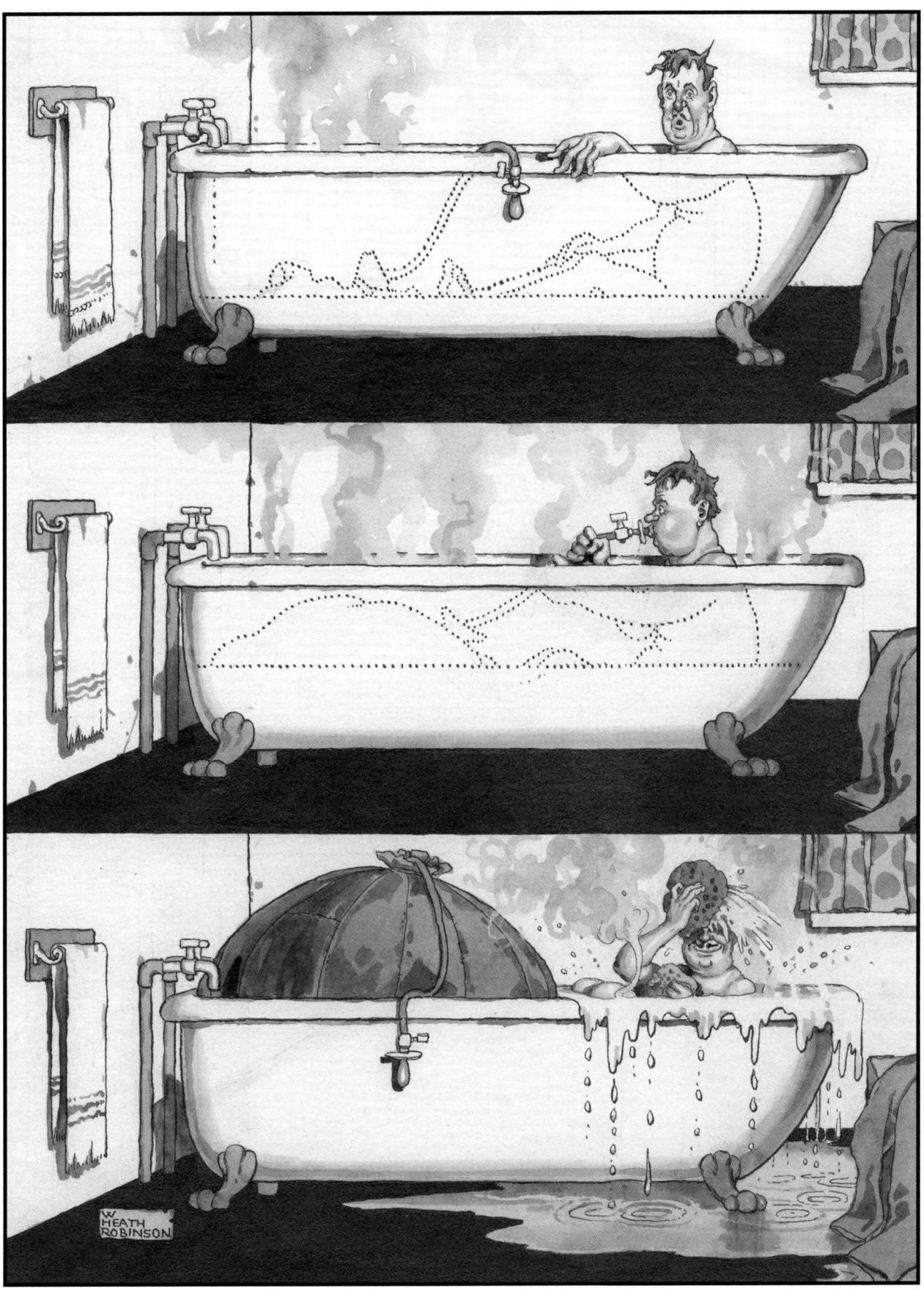

When the hot water tap runs cold: A new device for making a lot out of a little.

Testing Candidates – For the post of milk sourer at a cream cheese factory.

Aero-Chimney-Cleaning: The brainwave of an ex-captain of the RAF (Balloon Section).

Safety First: Prominent officials of the SPP (Society for the preservation of poultry) trying the effect of a new pullet preserver.

In Case They Strike: An intelligent suggestion in anticipation of cold mornings and coal shortage.

HEATH ROBINSON CONTRAPTIONS

From Heath Robinson Unlimited, the World Famous Manufacturers of "Glorious Gadgets":
Some really new Christmas presents.

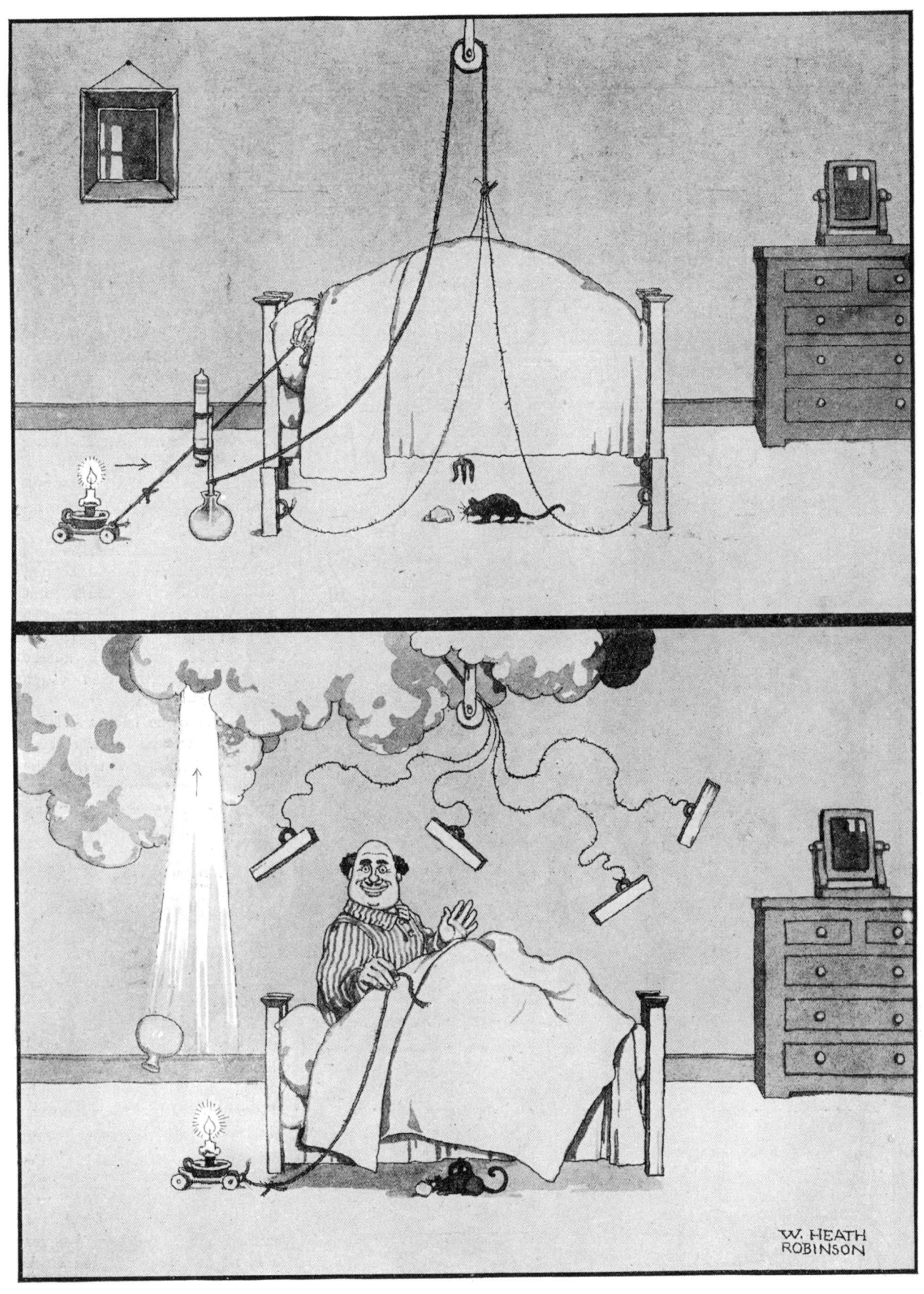

Straight from our Inventions Department: Rats – and how to catch them.

Latest Machine for tipping matches with phosphorus.

Bombing Tunny in the lagoons at Bude

Head Work! A new machine (adopted by some of our first-class restaurants) for putting a head on a glass of 1920-21 stout.

How it is Done: Completing a cricket bat handle in the winding grounds of a bat factory.

The Broadcaster – Picking up an aerial vibration.

HEATH ROBINSON CONTRAPTIONS

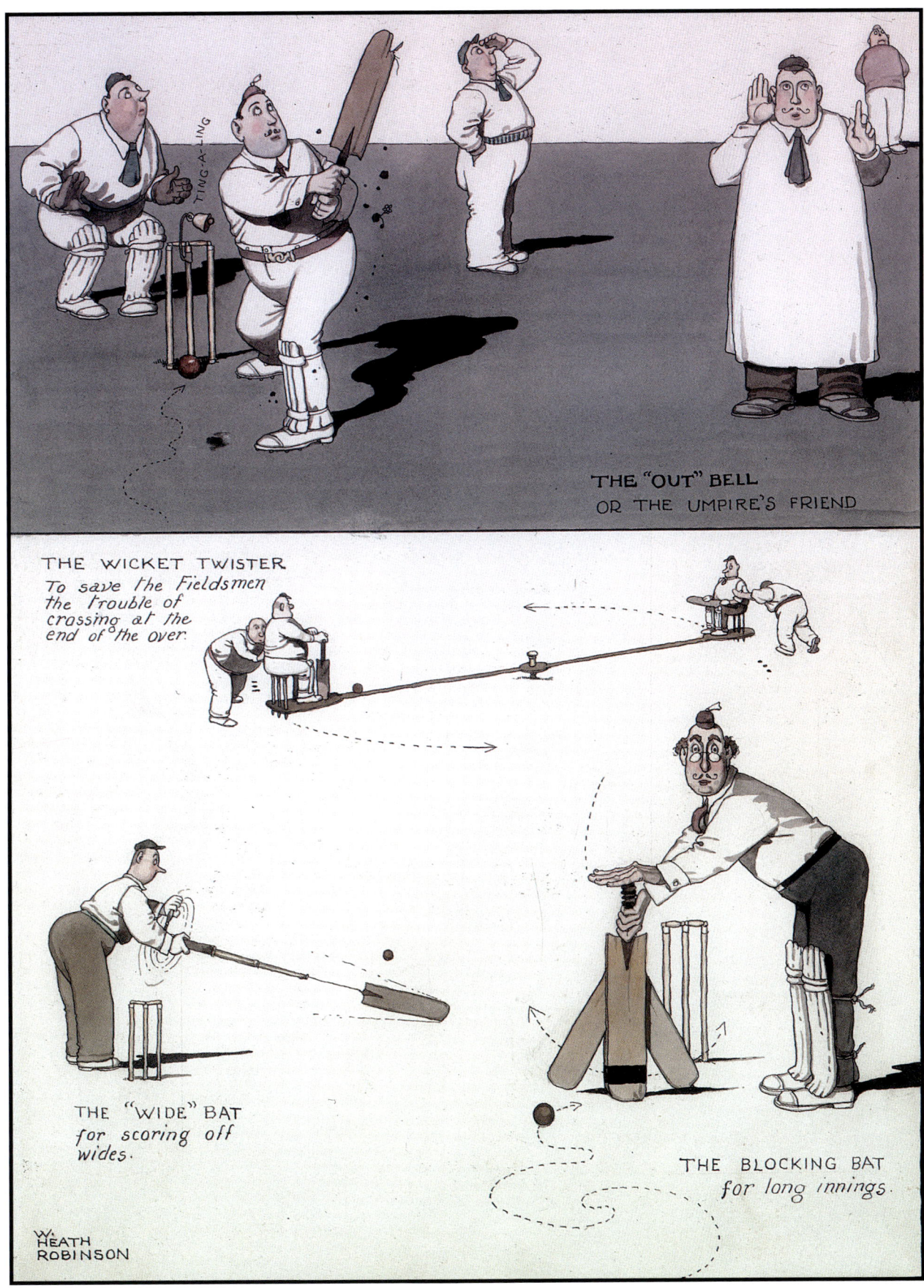

Some Cricket Novelties – to be Introduced Next Season – Official: For the assistance of fielders and batsmen.

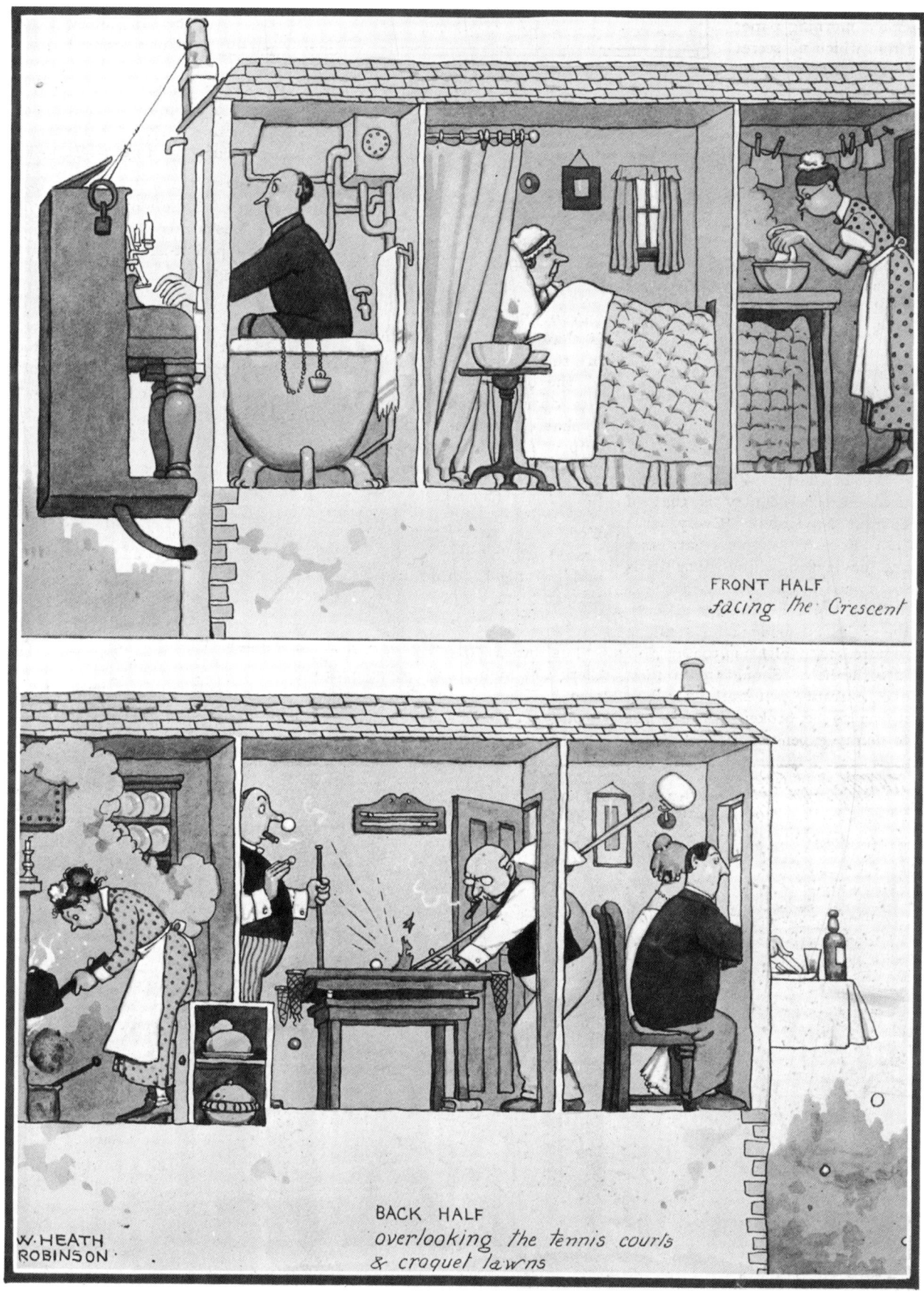

Heath Robinson Mansions W. – TO LET: Attractive flat containing:- Music-bath room; H&C bedroom; billiard room; dining room; kitchen; scullery; offices.

Would You be Beautiful? A few suggestions for the plain by a well known beauty specialist.

For next Season's Society Weddings: Testing the specific gravity of confetti before packing in one of our latest confetti mills.

Sew it Seams: In the cutting room of a gents' pyjama factory.

Self-help for Gardeners: How to prune a plum tree without a ladder.

– in the kitchen.

– in the dining room.

DOING AWAY WITH SERVANTS

– in the bedroom.

DOING AWAY WITH SERVANTS

– in the drawing room.

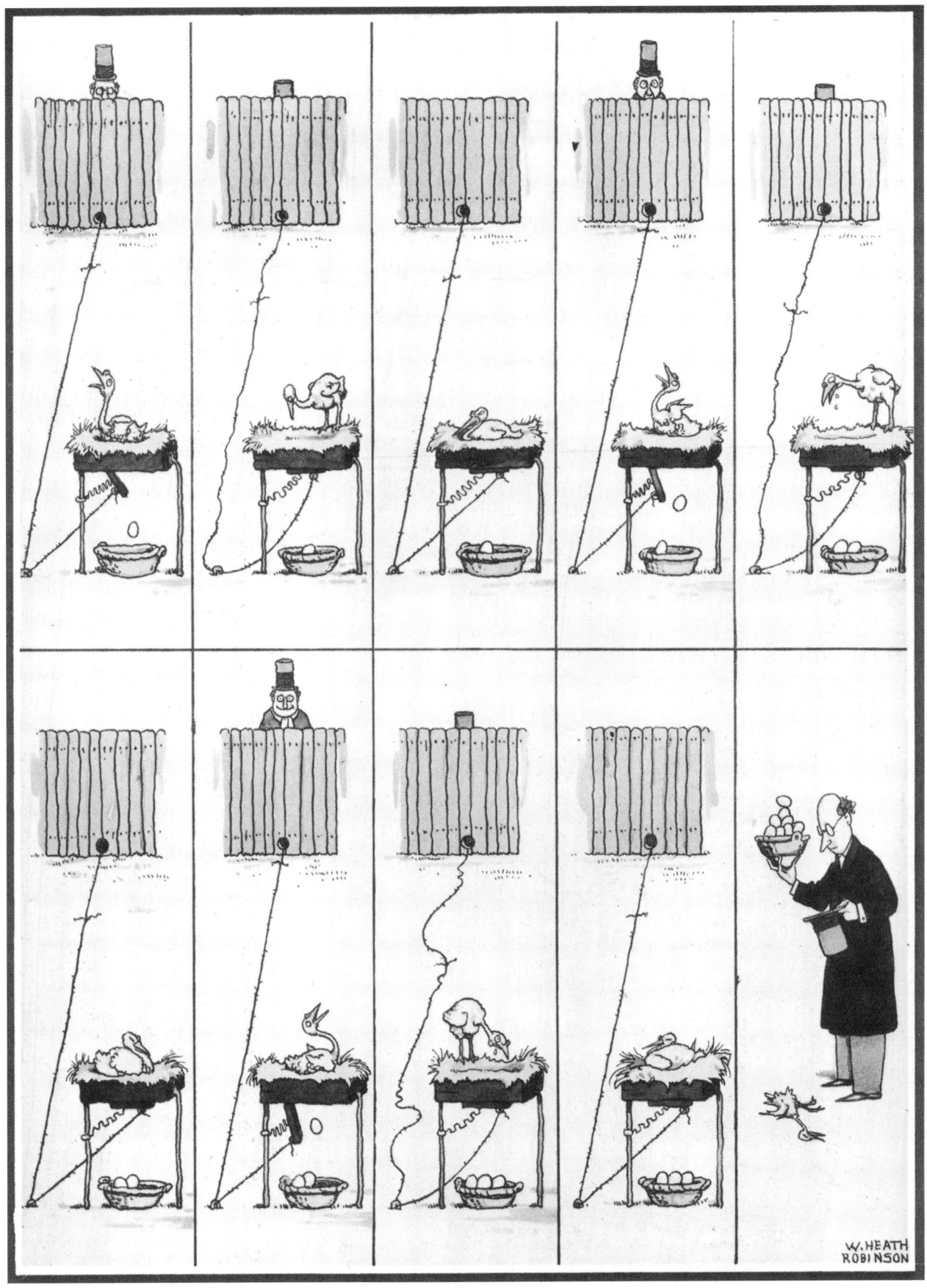

Mass Production: Forcing eggs for the London market.

Uncrossing the crosses on a Hot + Bun: Ingenious plant in an old bun works for smoothing out the crosses on the hot cross buns left over from Easter.

For Bashful Bachelors: The new portable wireless set for delicate propositions.
(Beware broadcasting!)

Round in One: Testing the bias of bowls at well-known sports factory.

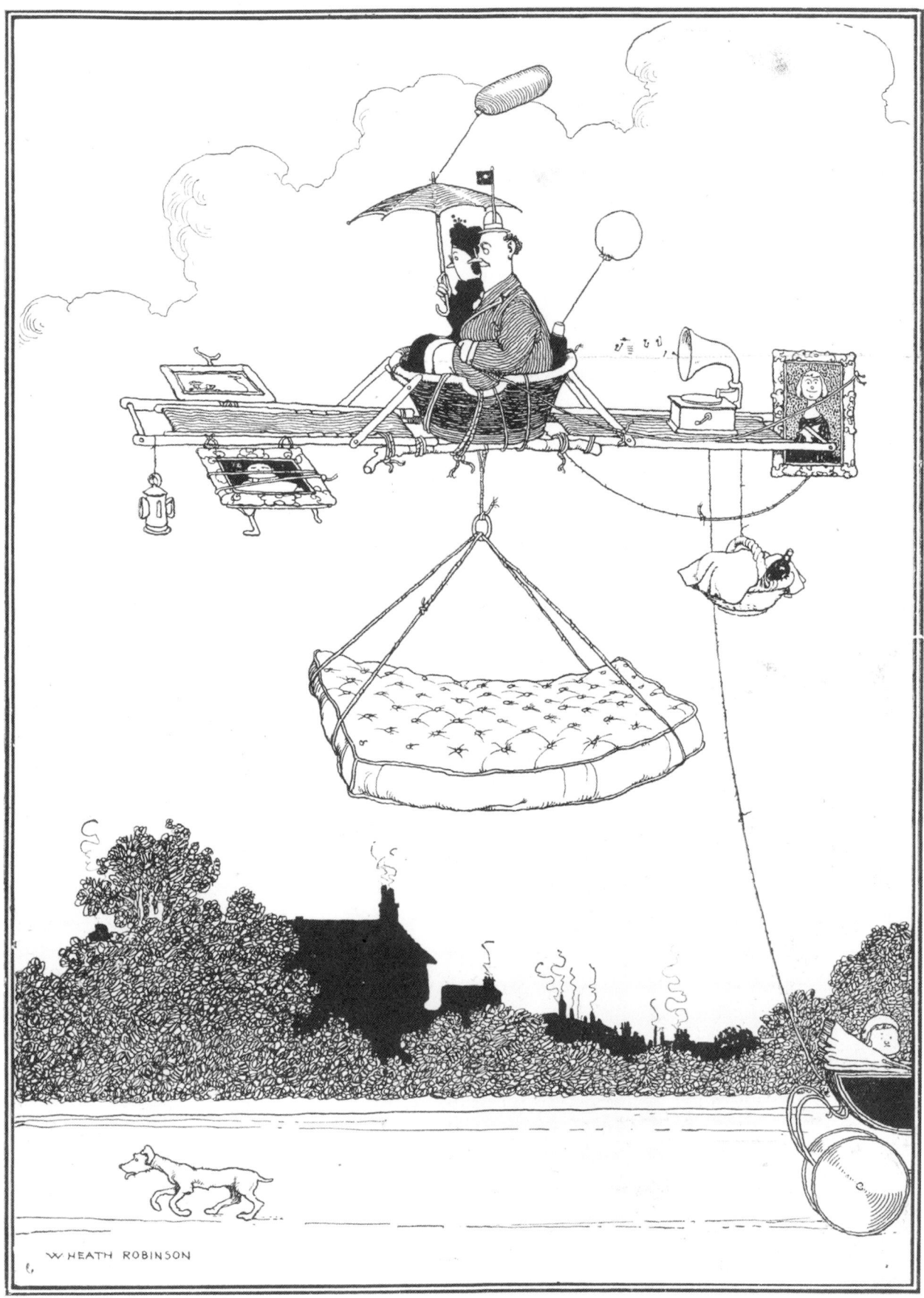

Safety First: The winner of the first prize offered by "The Bystander" for the best home made safety glider.

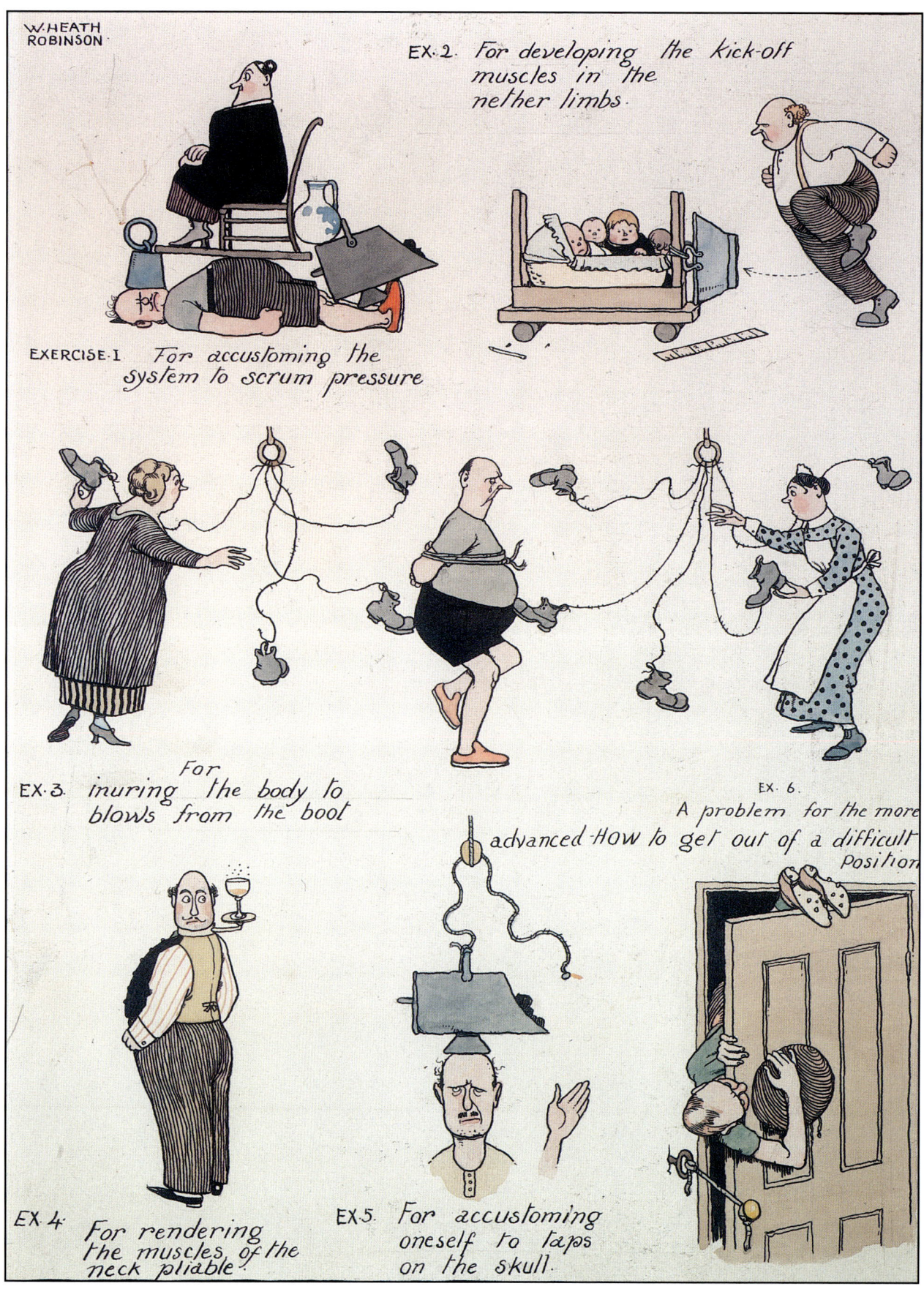

The Enthusiast: A short course of training for the rugger novice.

Consequences – How even a falling toothbrush may destroy the prospect of a happy Christmas.

A Great Grand Stand: A comfortable suggestion for viewing future royal weddings.

Relativity and all that sort of thing.

A Votive Offering: The canvassers' vade mecum.

His aeroplane

"I WAS EXCEEDINGLY SURPRISED WITH THE PRINT OF A MAN'S FOOT."

HIS WIRELESS.

"HOWEVER, AT LAST I TAUGHT HIM TO SPEAK."

His wireless

His home life

His submarine

His recreation

A Record Run: Filming the Indian tiger in his native haunts.

Quite Enough to Make One Reel: Filming a man-eating lion in the Libyan desert.

A Trunk Call: Intrepid film producer disguised as a currant bun, cinematographing wild elephants at play.

An Imperial Measure: The cunning contrivance of a denizen of Sheppey conveying his family to mainland en route for Wembley.

A link between the 19th century comic tradition and Heath Robinson's work can be found in the Volume of *Punch* for 1850. At page 109 is a drawing titled 'The advantage of lodging under a mechanical genius'. It shows a man being woken by having his bedclothes pulled off him. This is done by a cord that passes over a pulley and is attached to a heavy weight. The falling of the weight has been triggered by the clock on the wall reaching a specified time, and the weight has fallen with sufficient force to break through the floor, waking the man in the room below. This is, in simplified form, the archetypal Heath Robinson gadget, invented by an unidentified *Punch* artist about 60 years earlier.

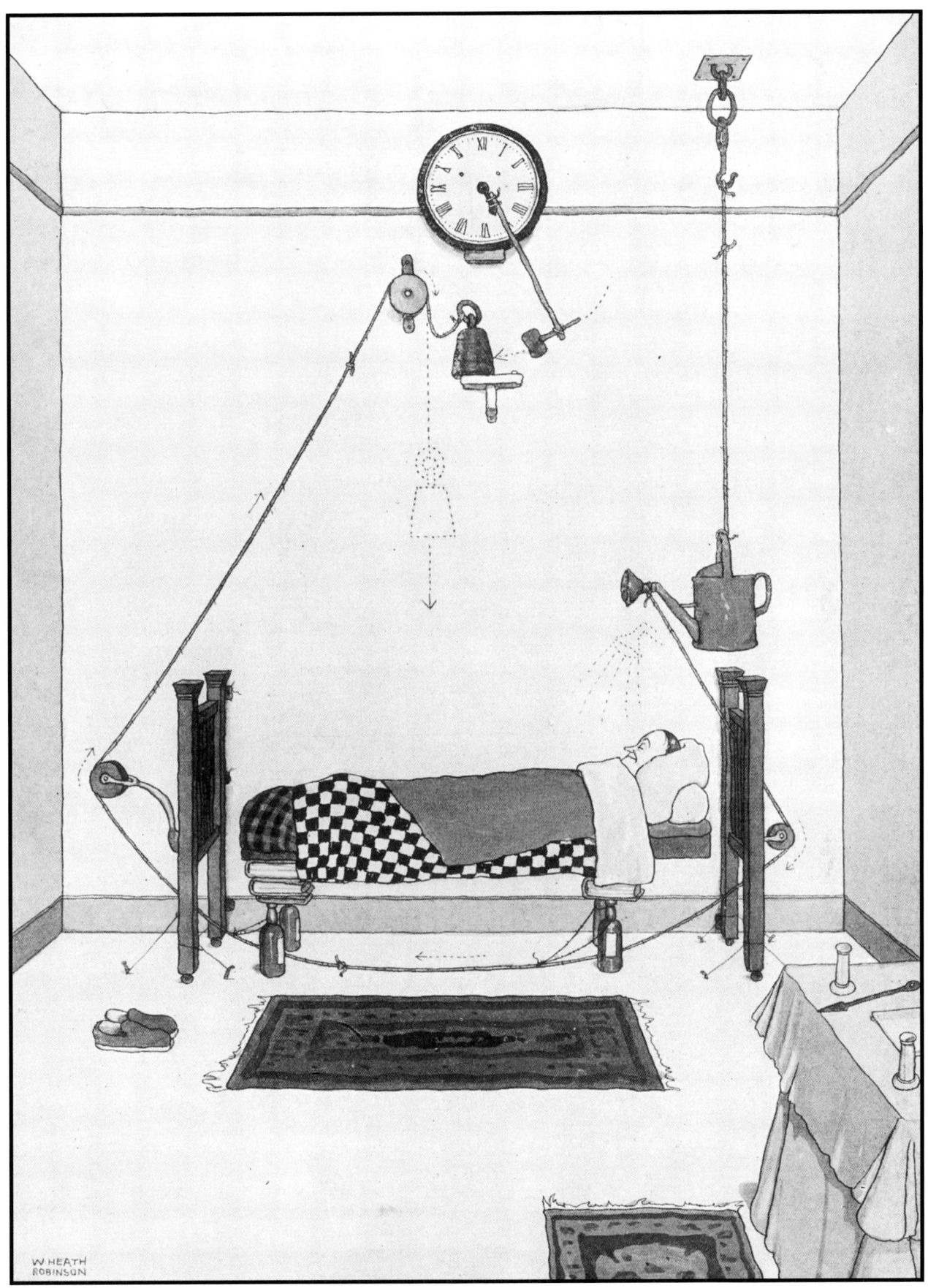

A Matter of the Moment: A simple expedient to accustom oneself to earlier rising in view of the near approach of Summer time.

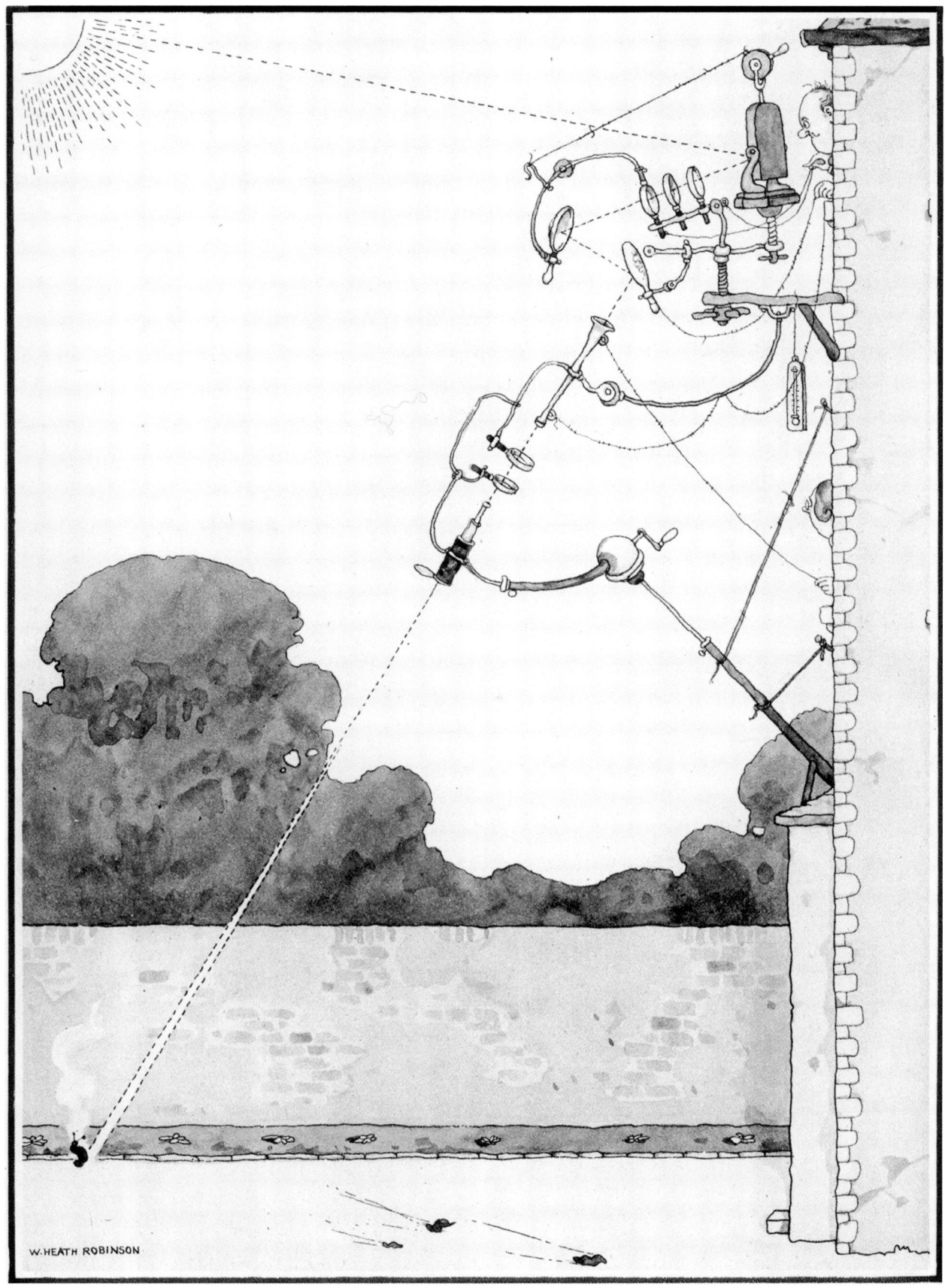

Hurray for the Robinson Ray! We are privileged to publish the first illustration of a Death Ray at its dirty work. The secret experiment was entirely successful and as our picture shows resulted in the slaughter of a slug from a top story window. (NB – The Government is still undecided as to the purchase of Mr HR's patent. Meanwhile, private offers will be considered.)

A High Court Ruling: The only really reliable way to test the correctness of the angles of your new lawn tennis court.

A Moving Scene at Wembley: Visitors to the British Empire Exhibition about to experience the thrills of the special earthquake machine devised by a well-known artist.

The Glass of Fashion: A pleasant fiction practised in upper circles when only a few of the invited guests turn up.

"The Merry, Merry Pipes of Pan-demonium": The multi-bagpipe for accompanying choral performances at society functions.

A Moving Cat-astrophe: A sectional view of a clever trap by which one of the "cat" burglars was lured to his doom.

A Bit of a Frost: A simple device for making your snow as you go along.

The Call of the Wild: A touching experiment in the early days of electric telephony – a pioneer endeavouring to hold a conversation with himself in his modest back garden.

A Time Saver for the Plane Business Man: How aviation enables the busy city man to get a sea dip between business appointments.

The man who forgot to take off the earphones.

Our Industrial Life – Making new potatoes from old in the spud department of Covent Garden.

"A Good Pull-up". The new electric self-raising braces for those men who haven't the time to fiddle about with the ordinary kind in the morning.

"The Aerocharrybang".

An Out and Out Success: A remarkable instance of a form of self-dentistry practised by thrifty business-men.

The Finer Points of Dancing: An ingenious device which allows the student to learn dancing in his home, and in particular to avoid treading on the toes of his partner.

Very Hot! The wonderful Heath Robinson new patent thawing machine. This stupendous invention has been specially designed to enable the pedestrian to walk with confidence on the most slippery roads.

A High Old Time: Testing the nerve of a promising young student at the Royal College of Steeplejacks.

Signs of Christmas – working overtime at the mint.

A Signal Invention: Intelligent method of overcoming difficulties of taking one's own photograph.

In the Merry, Merry Spring Time: The new Heath Robinson potato dibber for planting seed potatoes in the early spring.

Laying the foundation stone of the projected new London Bridge across the Thames.

Interesting sidelights on the wig industry (mass production for the million).

Potty: How our artist imagines that test cricketers secretly train in order to avoid being caught in any part of the field.

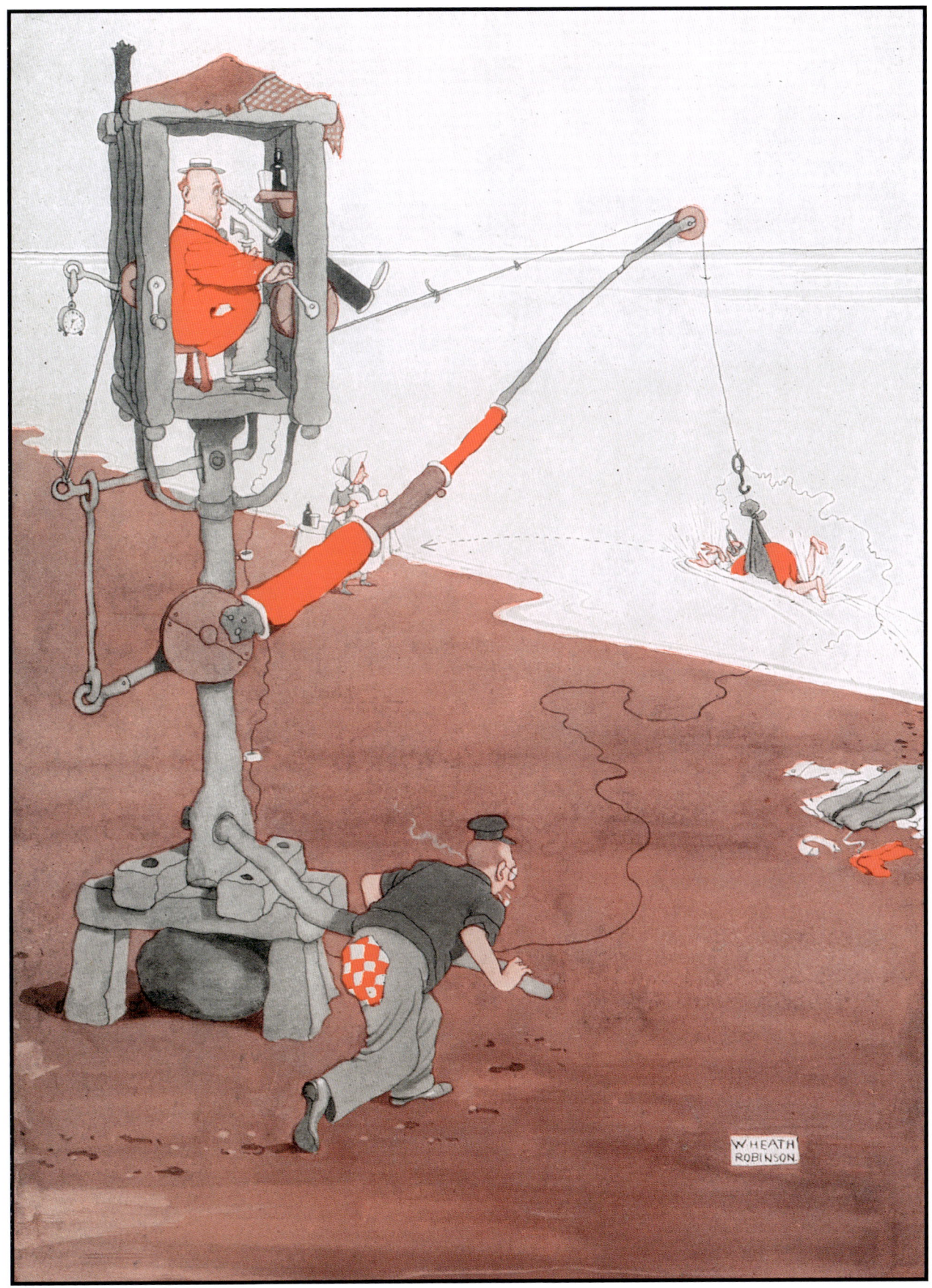

Lessons by Post: The new Heath Robinson swimming post which is acquiring such popularity at our most fashionable coast resorts.

"Our Rugged Island Brace". Testing the strength of British braces in one of our most important factories in the Midlands.

An Attractive Idea for Gents' Wear: Do you realise that the equinoctial gales will soon be blowing in upon us? If so do not forget to buy one of the new patent adjustable magnetic hat guards, for use with any style and size of hat.

Long Drawn Out! A simple home cure for warts.

Summer Tied: an ingenious method of prolonging summer adopted by a prominent inhabitant of South London.

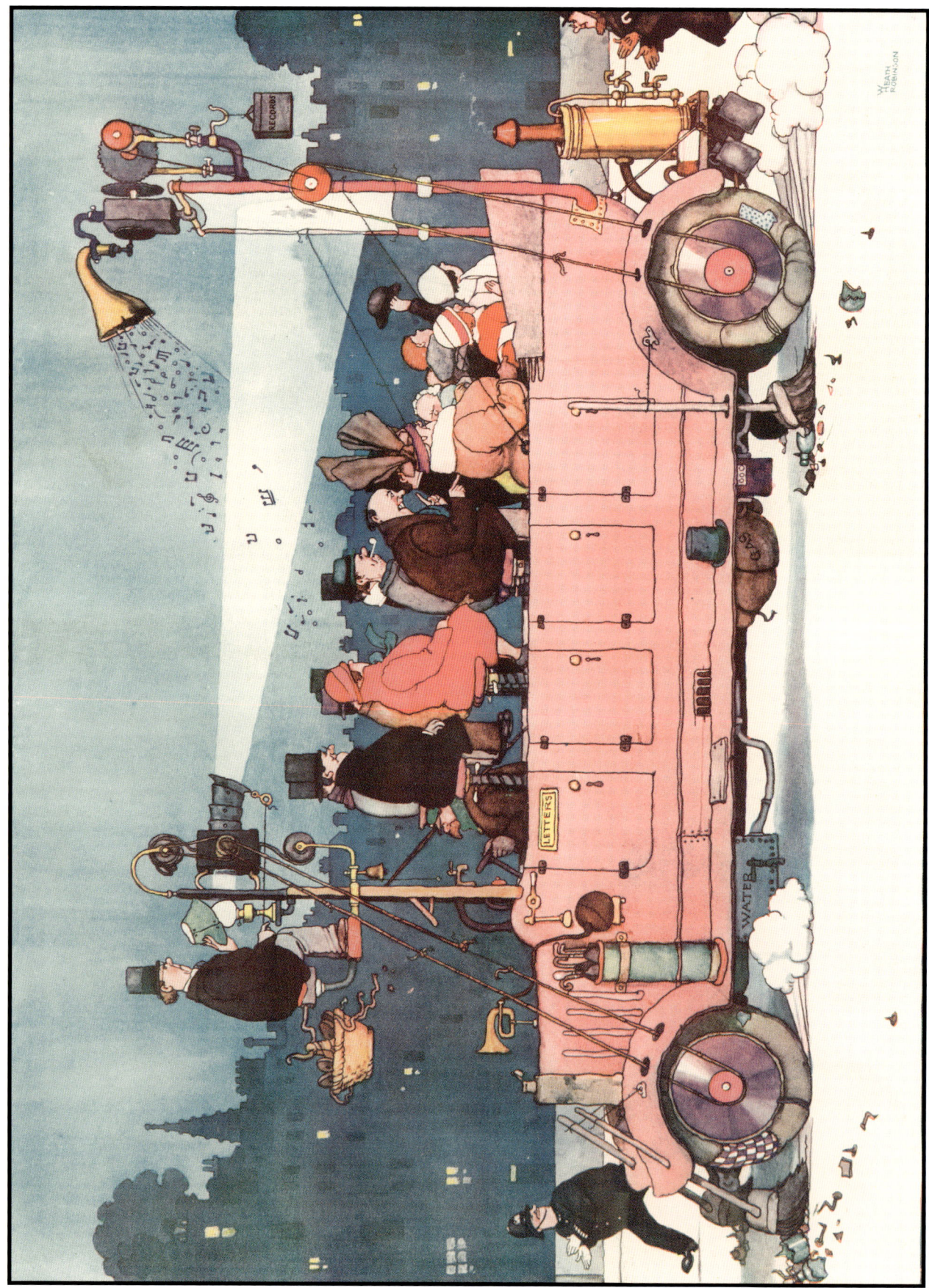

The Kinecar: An ingenious vehicle fitted with many devices for the comfort and amusement of passengers returning home on winter evenings.

Weighty Deeds Afoot – Testing Corn Plasters in the salon of a fashionable West End chiropodist.

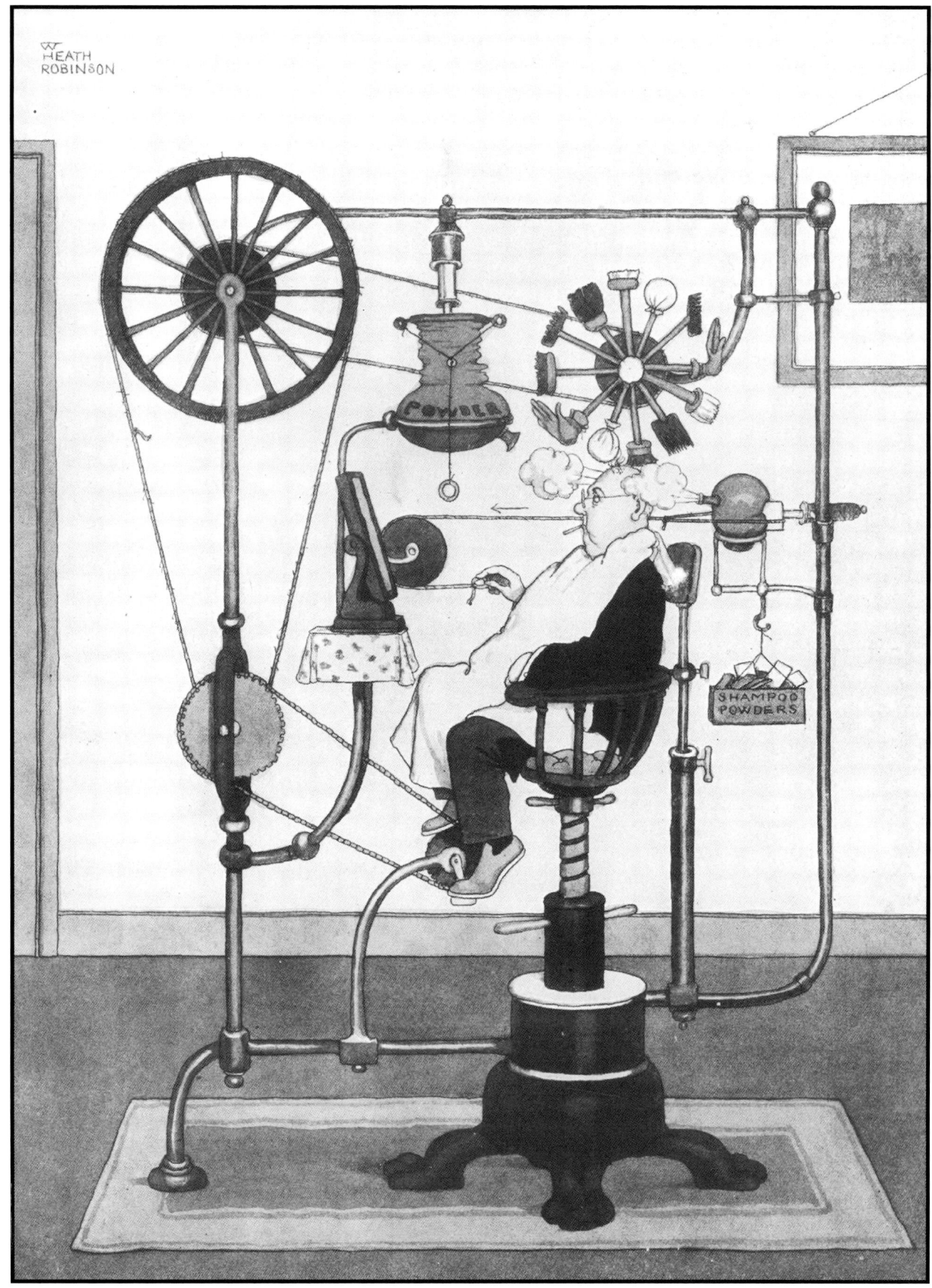

Hair Raising: The shampoo chair. A new invention for the convenience of those who prefer to do their own dry shampooing to entrusting their scalps to the tender mercies of the hairdresser.

An interesting afternoon with Mr Bryant and Mr May at their famous safety-match works.

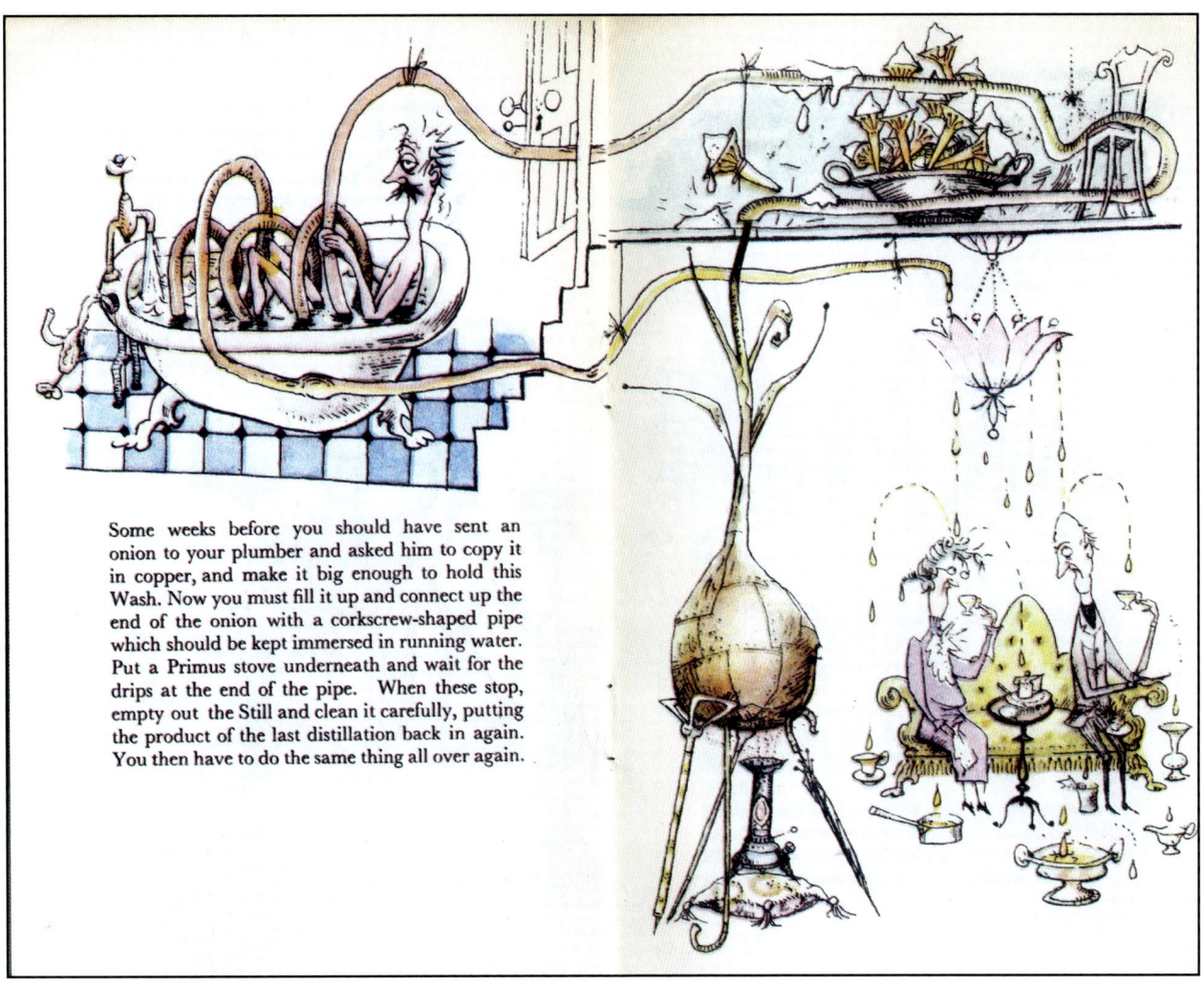

"Make Your Own Scotch Whisky", an illustration by Rowland Emett.

Rowland Emett (1906-1990) may be regarded as Heath Robinson's successor in the field of contraptions. He worked mainly for *Punch* drawing fantastic trains, trams and pleasure-steamers in a whimsical style, operated by aged, spindly figures. In 1951 his "Far Twittering to Oyster Creek Branch Line Railway", which had begun life as a series of drawings in *Punch* in 1944, was realised for the Festival of Britain, carrying over 2 million passengers.

"Well I'm Blowed!" The HR mark VII extra special pneumatic candle-flame extinguisher, specially devised for blowing the candle when the dressing table is a long way from the bed.
An ideal Christmas present. No home should be without one.

Wholly Unnecessary! One of the quaint old machines still occasionally to be met with in the wilder parts of Scotland for making the holes in Scottish golf courses.

Kept in Suspense: The new magnetic quicksand deck chair, a simple but reliable invention which enables one to sit on the more treacherous sands with perfect immunity.

The latest thing in tourist's outfits – specially recommended for walking tours.

"I Passed by Your Window"! The modesty blind, which will be welcomed for dealing with delicate situations at the seaside.

Good Man! Alarmingly successful result of an early endeavour to construct a home-made robot.

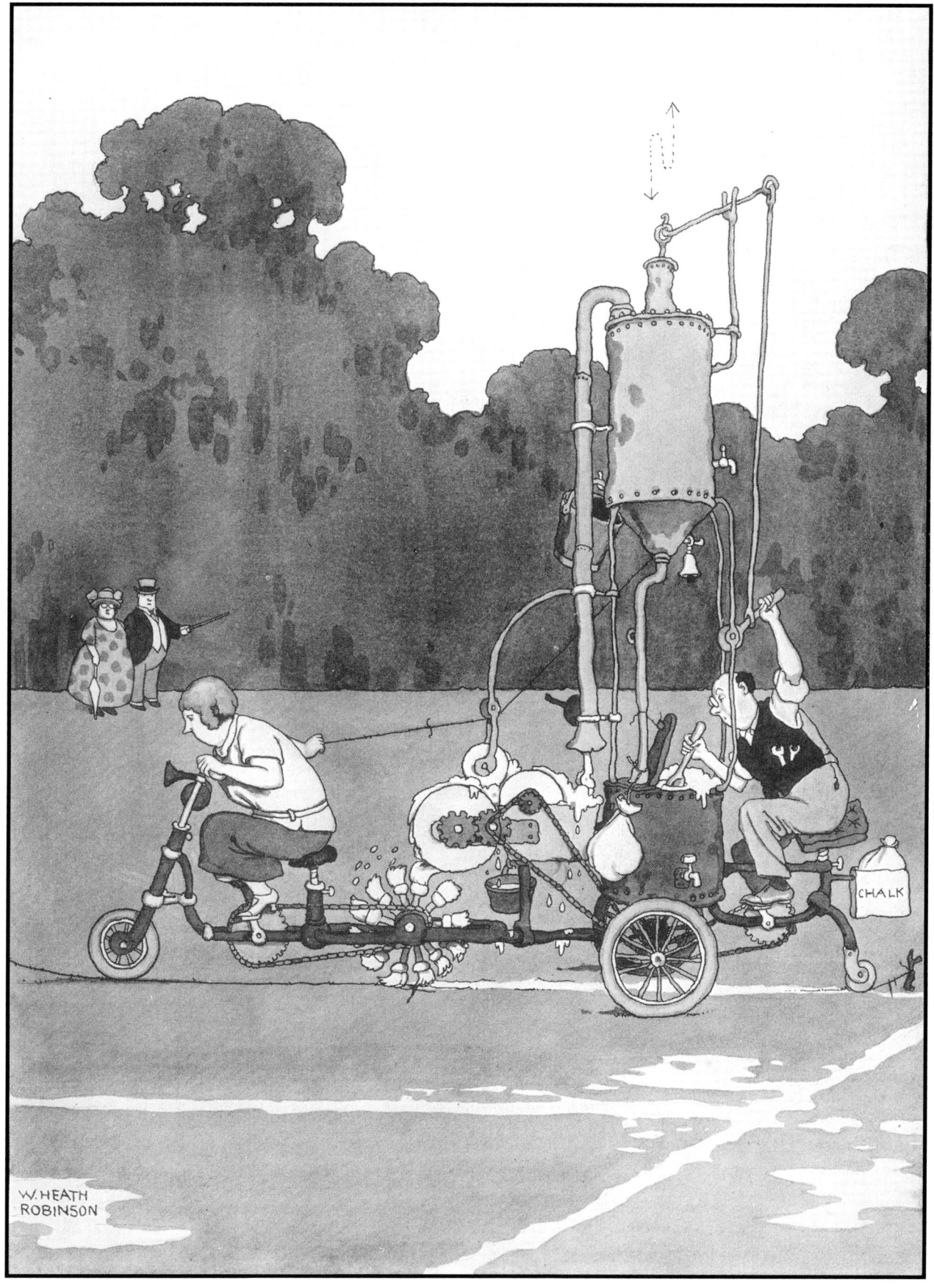

A Marker of Mark on the Market: A new labour saving lawn marker which is the sensation of the lawn tennis world. Requiring only two people to operate it, there is no doubt that it will soon be found in every up-to-date establishment.

Magnetic aids for skaters.

A Decided Catch: The whitebait cycle. An ingenious contraption necessitated by the exorbitant charges for the hire of boats at the seaside this season.

A Seaside Snap Shot: Ingenious method of overcoming the difficulty of taking one's own photograph while bathing.

The broadcast play – how they produce the sound effects.

Ups-a-Daisy! A sensible provision now made on some of the nursery slopes, whereby the plump skier may, with the minimum of effort, regain his or her feet after a fall.

Ending in Smoke: An ingenious smoke-screen spreader for preventing embarrassing situations when the bathroom lock is out of order.

Ingenious device of a highland wait for dealing with Scottish boarding houses on Christmas Eve.

Weight and See: The new safety ice tester for testing under comfortable conditions the capacity of the ice to bear the weight of the average British citizen.

The Frame Up: One of the new training frames for instructing young cat burglars in the art of overcoming obstacles in their path.

"You'll Come to It by Degrees": Do you find your cold dip too much of a shock these nippy mornings?
If so, why not try the gradual approach from hot to cold in the above way,
which is strongly recommended by the bathing faculty.

George Cruikshank – "Overhead and underfoot".

While the majority of Heath Robinson's humorous drawings are entirely fresh and original, it is sometimes possible to find the inspiration for his work in the classic 19th century humorous tradition. The origin of his delightful 'Savoy Orpheans' drawing lies in George Cruikshank's Comic Almanac for 1837. This includes a plate titled 'Over-head and Under-foot' showing four young blades carousing in an upstairs room, jumping and stamping around. In the room below their neighbour, looking extremely miserable, sits waiting for the noise to stop, so that he can retire to his bed, which is seen through an open door. Heath Robinson has taken this composition, with the two rooms, one above the other, seen in cross-section, and has used it to show how considerate of their neighbours people can be. In the upper room a party of over 20 people are dancing vigorously to the BBC's broadcast of the Savoy Orphean Dance Music, but they have taken precautions to ensure that their neighbour in the room below is not disturbed. There are mattresses on the floor, the dancers' feet are muffled in various ways, and the music is heard through individual earphones. While the neighbour in Cruikshank's picture is having a miserable time, Heath Robinson's neighbour is sleeping soundly.

How to take advantage of the Savoy Orpheans dance music broadcast by the BBC without disturbing the neighbour in the flat below.

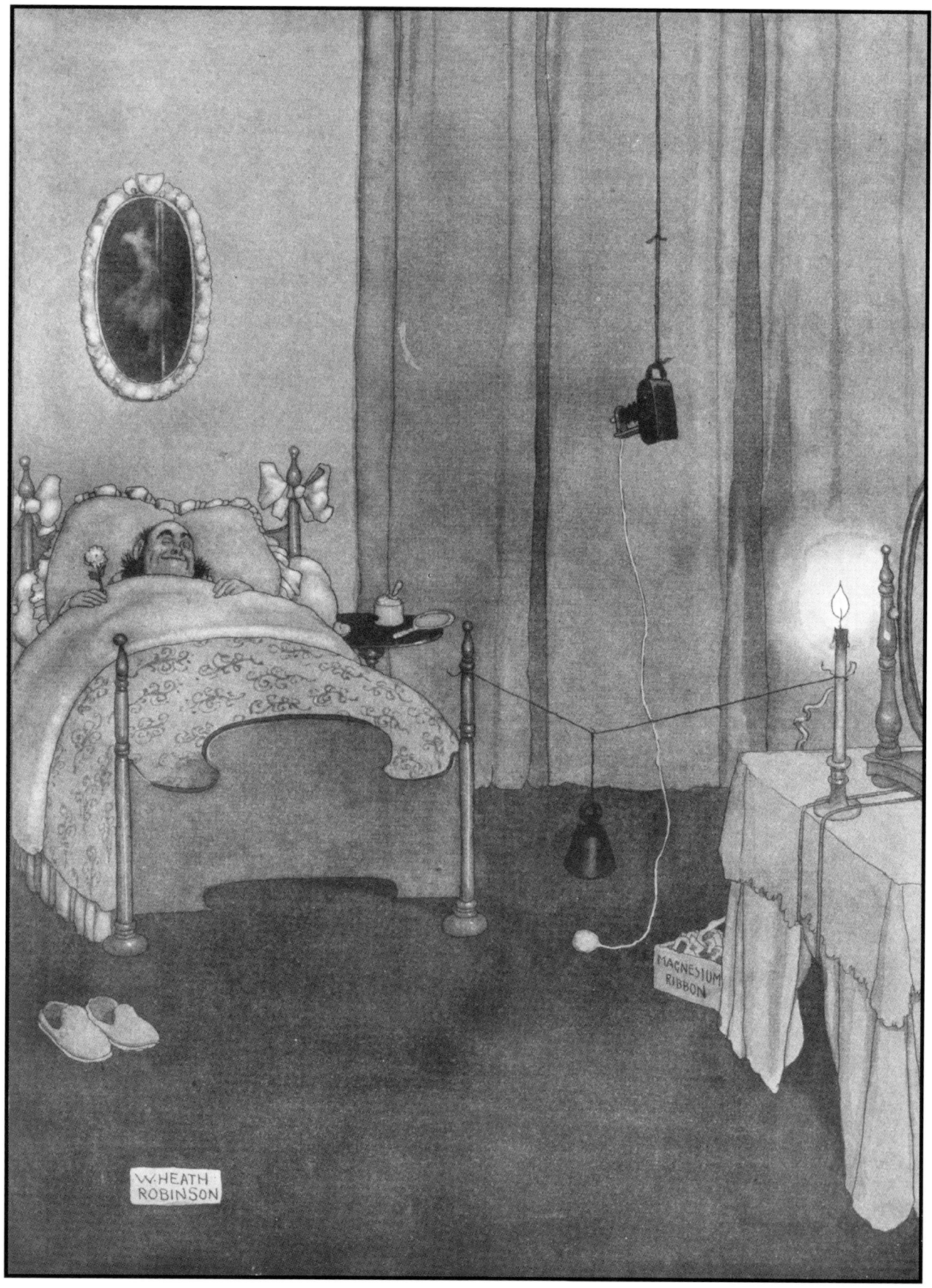

"Sleep, my Pretty One, Sleep!" How one of the many enquiring minds who wonder what they look like when asleep satisfied his curiosity.

Sandpaper chute for removing the shine from blue serge trousers.

The homemade Turkish bath.

Spring cleaning in Aberdeen.

Testing artificial teeth in a modern tooth works.

Pea Eating Extraordinary. An elegant and interesting apparatus designed to overcome once and for all the difficulties of conveying green peas to the mouth.

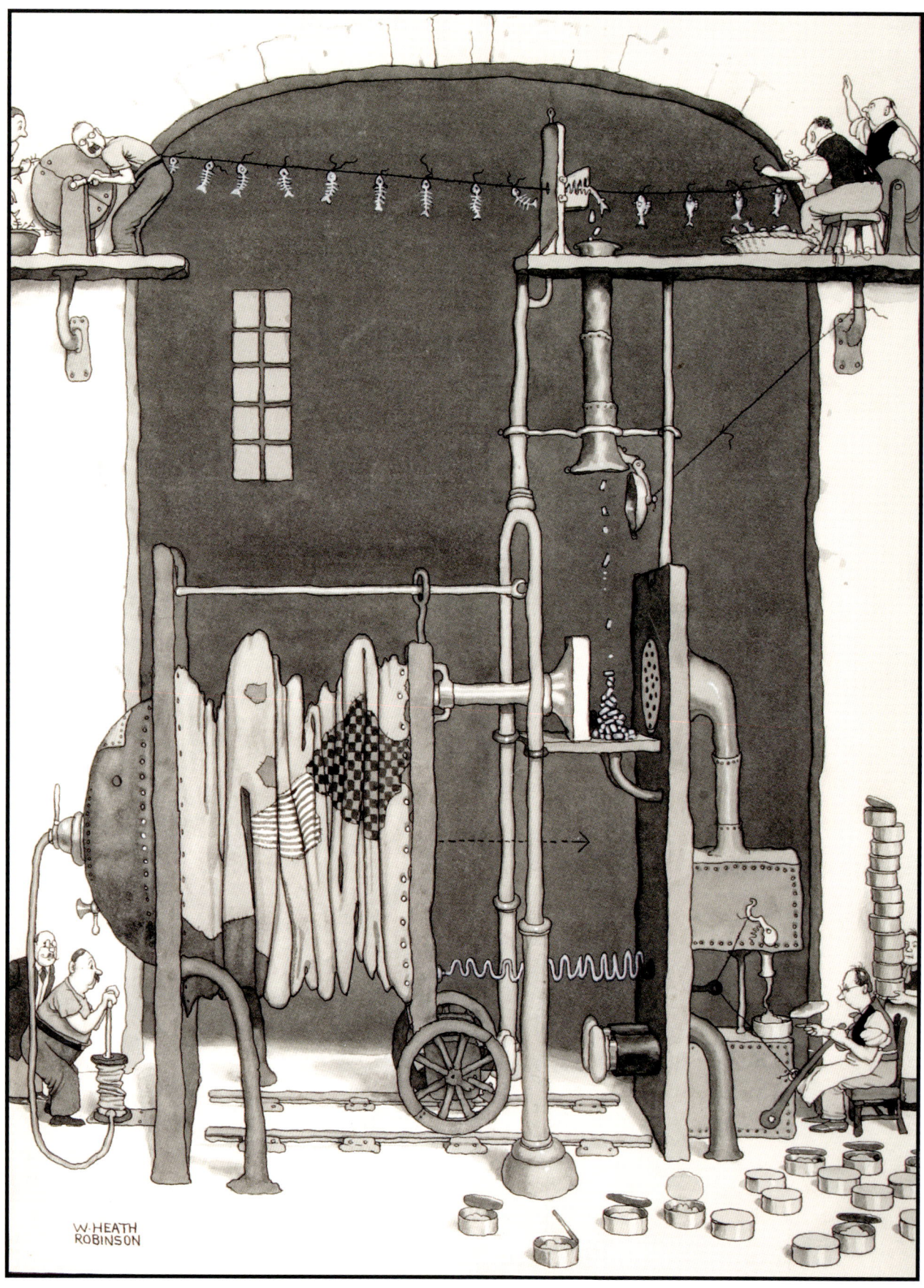

The new salmon squeezer fitted with patent filleter.

The flat of the future.

A new method of teaching would-be anglers to angle.

Frantic efforts of the last man at the sea side.

Putting the tartan on kilts in an old kilt works.

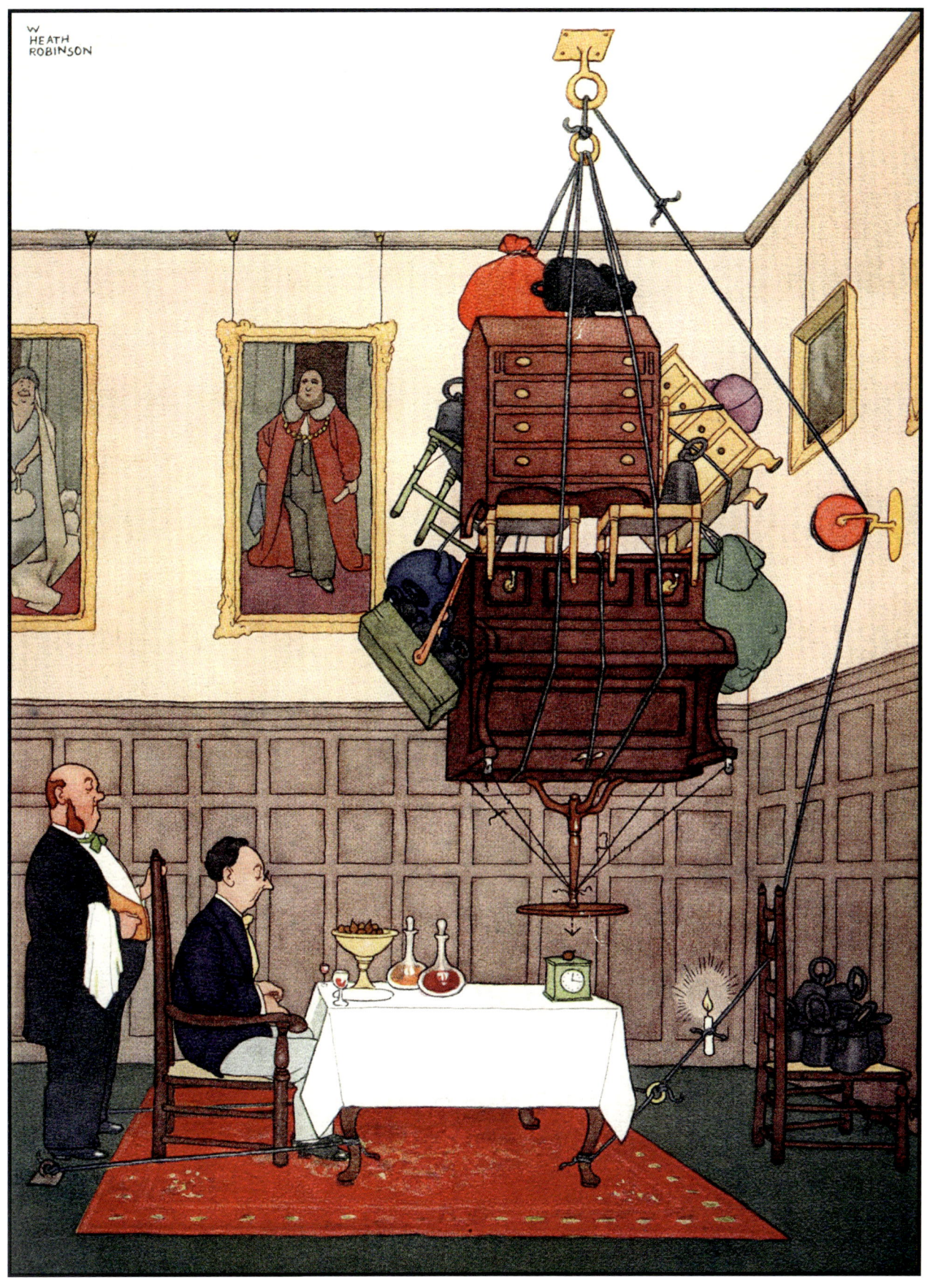

"Everything comes to him who waits." A simple method of cracking nuts.

"Fire is a good servant but a bad master." An elegant apparatus for lighting a cigar in safety.

"It takes two to make a quarrel." How to smooth over those little differences that sometimes occur in Bridge.

"Two's company, three's none." Sensible precaution against sudden interruption of confidential conversation.

"All's fair in love and war." A cleverly planned elopement.

"Early to bed and early to rise etc., etc." An ingenious device for getting up in good time in the morning.

No. 1 – Bedroom Comfort.

AN IDEAL HOME

No. 2 – The folding garden.

No. 3 – Space economy at a wedding.

AN IDEAL HOME

No. 4 – Top Floor Chicken Farm.

AN IDEAL HOME

No. 5 – The spare room.

AN IDEAL HOME

No. 6 – Sports without broad acres.

"The Gadgets" with Heath Robinson at the lower right in the trilby hat.

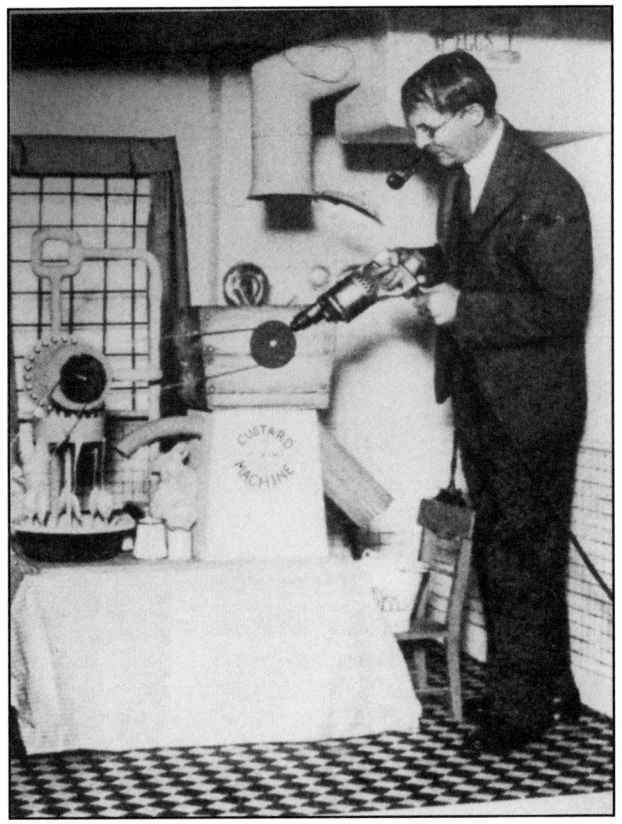

Putting the finishing touches to the custard mixing machine.

To Heath Robinson 1934 was a memorable year. It saw the creation at the "Ideal Home Exhibition" at Olympia of his ideal home, "The Gadgets". The house stood on a site 50ft by 30ft and was nearly 20ft high. It was peopled with more than thirty life-like moving figures, all busy about their daily tasks. Father, mother, baby, nurse – each was modelled by the engineering firm of Veranco Ltd, under the supervision of their creator, to a scale of half life-size. Each too was said to be fitted for clothes of a fashionable kind, although to whose idea of fashion is not quite clear. The visitor could see the family in action from the time they were woken in the morning until they retired at night. Father and mother dropping through the bedroom floor to the dining room beneath on the end of counter-balanced ropes would, by so doing, turn on the radio-gramophone, give the cat its milk and uncover the breakfast sausages. He was now indeed the Gadget King!

The Gadgets

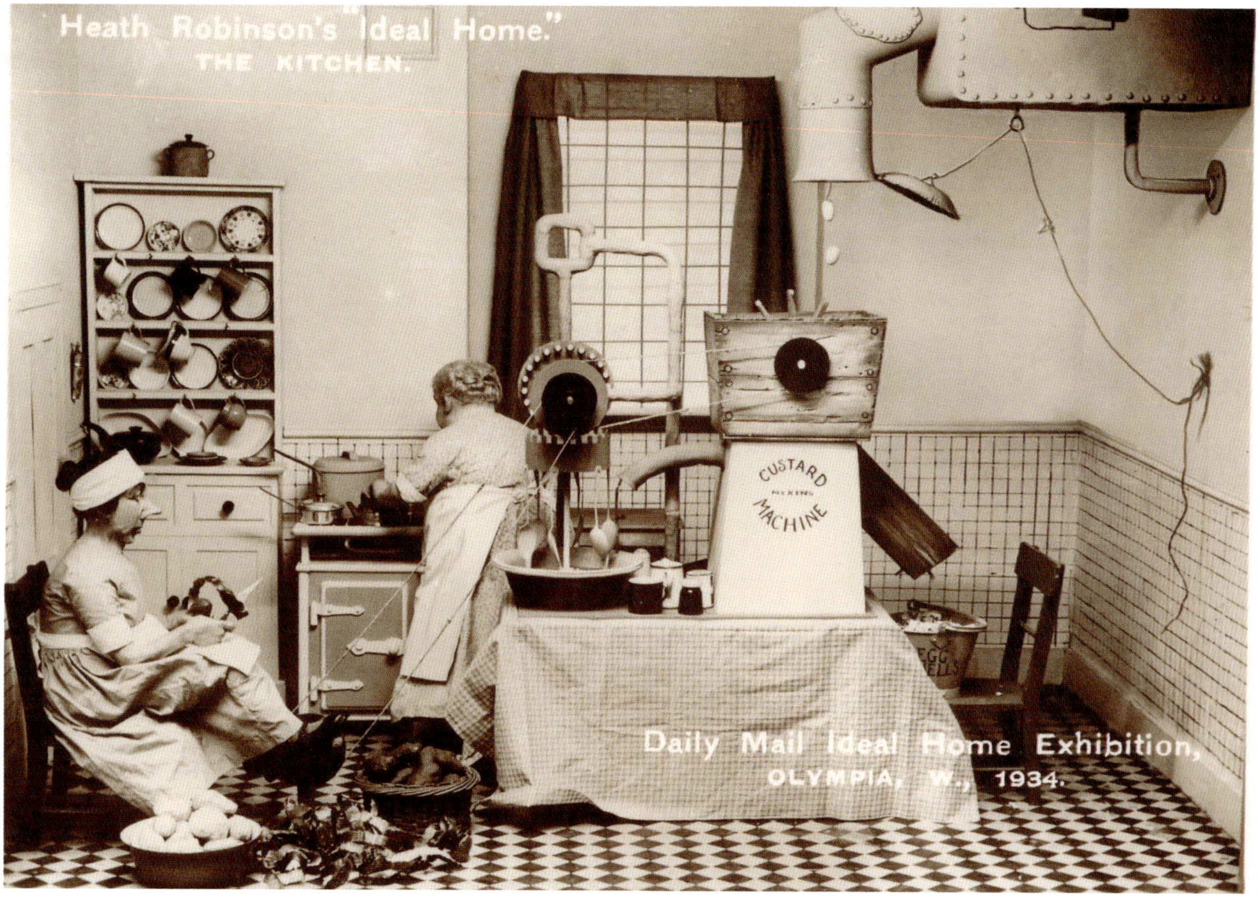

The Kitchen

HEATH ROBINSON'S IDEAL HOME

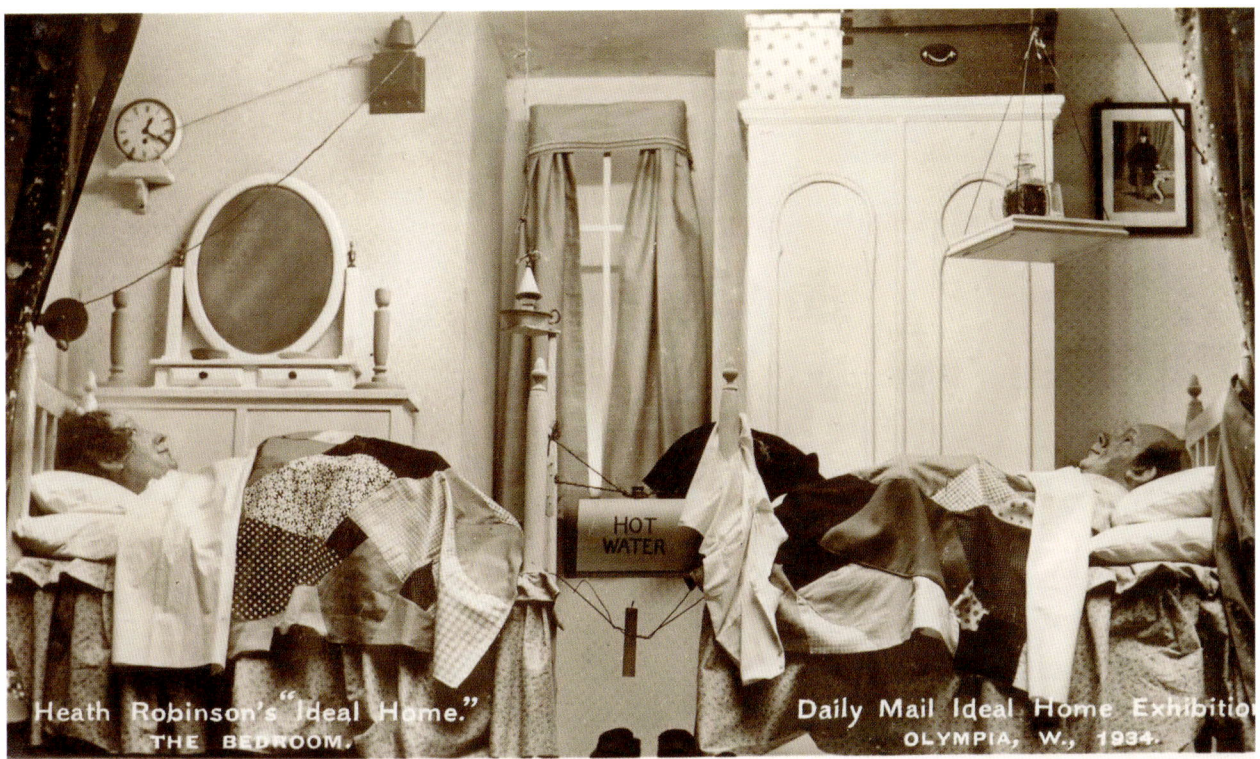

The Bedroom

The Dining Room

163

The Nursery

The Garden

HEATH ROBINSON CONTRAPTIONS

Space economy in a suburban maisonette.

"*To Mr. Heath Robinson, a pair of old motor-tyres is a hammock in embryo.*"

IT is fairly common knowledge that in the year 1666 Sir Isaac Newton was hit on the head by an apple, with momentous consequences to all mankind. It is less widely known, I think, that before rushing indoors to invent the Law of Averages, the venerable sage paused to devour the inspiring fruit, whimsically remarking: "Wayste notte, wante notte."

One feels that Sir Isaac would have found much in common with Mr. W. Heath Robinson, in whom the anti-waste instinct is so strongly developed as to be almost visible. Mr. Heath Robinson's inventive faculty has given delight to millions; but fully to appreciate his genius it is necessary to visit his home and observe how skilfully he has employed his talents to solve the little problems of everyday life. If wilful waste makes woeful want, woeful want is one thing that will never keep him awake at night.

AT HOME WITH HEATH ROBINSON

By K. R. G. BROWNE

It would seem that there is nothing so old, so decrepit, or so apparently useless that its possibilities escape Mr. Heath Robinson's shrewd eye. Things that even an Aberdonian housewife would throw to the dog or set aside as Christmas presents for her poorer relatives are eagerly seized by him and put to uses undreamed-of by their original designers. Whether or no he is genealogically connected with those well-known castaways, the Swiss Family Robinson and the late Mr. Robinson Crusoe, I hold that his ingenuity transcends even theirs; for the Swiss outfit received a good deal of assistance from Providence, while Mr. Crusoe was content to satisfy only his most elementary needs.

For example: did it ever occur to the Swiss Family Robinson that an old silk hat, carefully waterproofed, fitted with a little doorway and mounted on a disused clothes-prop, would make a charming dovecot for the front garden? Did Mr. Crusoe

"*A hand-made mirror which any lady would be proud to peer at.*"

At Home with Heath Robinson

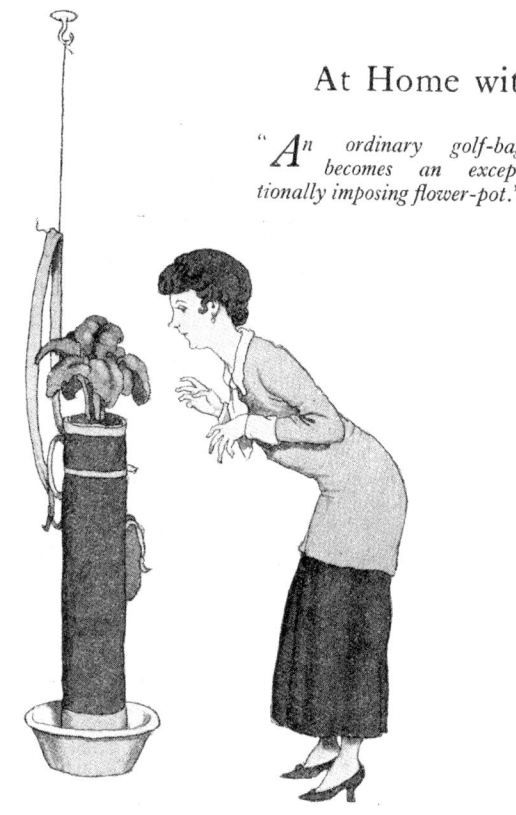

"*An ordinary golf-bag becomes an exceptionally imposing flower-pot.*"

ever realise that door-knockers, of a kind at once pleasing to the eye and diverting to the postman, can be contrived from superannuated briar pipes ? I doubt it ; but Mr. Heath Robinson has not only conceived these ideas, but acted on them, with the result that it is a positive pleasure to deliver a parcel at his address, while birds wishing to spend a few days on his premises must await their turn in a queue.

The foregoing are typical manifestations of the Heath Robinson code, which lays it down that practically anything can be converted, with a little thought and industry, into practically anything else, and vice versa. It follows that a visit to the Heath Robinson homestead is an education in the art of utilising the unexpected. At every turn the visitor is confronted by some familiar object fulfilling an unfamiliar function, such as—to pluck a brace of samples at random from the bag—the motor-tyre-picture-frame and the umbrella-parrot-cage.

What is the ordinary man's reaction to such flotsam as old motor-tyres and coverless umbrellas ? A motor-tyre by the river's brim a simple motor-tyre is to him, and it is nothing more. As for coverless umbrellas—other than those having gold-mounted handles—these have no message for him.

With Mr. Heath Robinson it is far otherwise. To him, a pair of old motor-tyres is anything from a hammock in embryo to a potential couple of picture-

"*Hats, handbags, even perambulator-wheels are among the reincarnations in which old gramophone records are likely to appear.*"

68

K. R. G. Browne

frames. Show him a coverless umbrella and watch his eye light up, as he reflects that a few bits of string and the base of an old ale-cask are all that is needed to convert it into a decorative parrot's cage. (If one has no parrot at the time, so much the better. Mr. Heath Robinson's method of building the cage first and then deciding to buy a parrot is obviously more sensible than the old-fashioned practice of acquiring the fowl first and erecting the cage around it.)

It may be argued by the thoughtless that old motor-tyres simply *cannot* be such stuff as picture frames are made of. To which I can only reply that, if we all had the courage of Mr. Heath Robinson's convictions, they emphatically *would* be. Only those who have been privileged to view his handiwork can appreciate how greatly an old motor-tyre enhances the appeal of the average oil-portrait or coloured photograph. Enshrined in solid rubber, even Great-Aunt Emmeline—who expired in 1897, a martyr to ingrowing disapproval—takes on a kind of faery charm, to the surprise of all who knew her.

For his solution of the aspidistra difficulty alone, Mr. Heath Robinson deserves the cordial thanks of all who are forced by cruel circumstance to cohabit with one of those grim vegetables. At its best—which it very seldom is—the aspidistra is no thing of beauty; and as customarily potted (i.e. in a sort of pink china soup-tureen) it looks even worse. It has been left to Mr. Heath Robinson to perceive that an ordinary golf-bag, when emptied of niblicks, etc., filled with loam and stood upright in a corner of the dining-room, becomes an exceptionally imposing flower-pot in which an aspidistra looks less like an aspidistra than one would think possible. I may be wrong, but my impression is that men

"*A shapely cake-stand constructed almost entirely of old fox-trots and cornet solos.*"

"*Fitted with a handle, and abbreviated, old trousers make excellent butterfly-nets.*"

At Home with Heath Robinson

have won medals for smaller services to the nation.

Ah, but what—the intelligent reader may inquire, after working it out on his cuff—if Mr. Heath Robinson wishes to play golf? Lacking a golf-bag, how can he battle with Bogey? Well, that is just one of those cases where genius will out. A lesser man, having sacrificed his golf-bag in the interests of suffering humanity, would probably give up golf and adopt some more portable pastime, such as halma.

Not so Mr. Heath Robinson. What—he reasons, in effect—are old trousers for? Merely to be carved into paint-rags, degraded to dusterhood, or employed to mop up milk-stains from the floors of ballrooms? No, no, a thousand times no! Stiffen their upper orifice, or waist-hole, with strong wire, tie up each lower aperture, or shin-vent, with stout twine—and there is a unique double golf-bag in neat blue serge or gentlemanly tweed. One leg should be allotted to the wooden clubs, the other to the irons; and even the braces, as the illustration shows, can play their part in the transformation.

From golf to entomology is a longish step for all except this remarkable man. To his keen eye it was at once apparent that, abbreviated as requisite, treated as above and fitted with a handle, old trousers also make excellent butterfly-nets for non-golfing naturalists. Persons desiring simultaneously to play golf and chase butterflies cannot, unfortunately, have it both ways; but not even Mr. Heath Robinson can think of everything It should suffice that he has given our old trousers a new lease of life and brought butterfly-hunting within the reach of the most penurious.

It was his success with this experiment, I imagine, that inspired Mr. Heath Robinson to invent his admirable Hand-Mirror For Large-ish Ladies. Ordinarily, there is nothing quite so useless as an old tennis-racket. Except when used for swatting flies or in amateur shrimping bouts, it lies forlornly

"*A unique double golf-bag in neat blue serge or gentlemanly tweed.*"

K. R. G. Browne

"*G*arden-shears can be contrived by anybody having a lot of old razor-blades."

about the house, trapping the unwary foot and getting generally in the way. The only house it does not lie about is Mr. Heath Robinson's, for he long ago discovered that by wrenching out the knitted portion and refilling the resultant vacuum with looking-glass, he could convert an old tennis-racket into a hand-mirror which any lady of quality would be proud to peer lovingly at.

And even that is not the sum of our artist's inventive activities. It is rather chastening to have to report that he, alone among men, has found a use for (*a*) old gramophone records and (*b*) electric bulbs which have gone permanently out, doubtless fusing several others in so doing. The average citizen's method of dealing with such jetsam is to park it casually in cupboards until the shelves give way under its weight, when he summons the local jetsam-merchant and has it laboriously removed.

Domestic inefficiency of that kind is simply incomprehensible to Mr. Heath Robinson. Take tea with him, and you will receive your currant bun from a shapely cake-stand constructed almost entirely of old double-sided fox-trots and cornet solos, now happily silent for ever. Should you feel the heat, you will be offered an obsolete violin concerto, cunningly adapted for use as a fan. Hats, hand-bags, card-trays, even perambulator-wheels—these are but a few of the reincarnations in which old gramophone records are liable to appear if Mr. Heath Robinson is anywhere about.

(Even his garden spade, I understand, was once the First Movement of an oratorio which, when performed at the Albert Hall in 1912, evoked shrill pæans from the critics and was faintly audible in Bayswater.)

As for electric bulbs, spare a glance for Mr. Heath Robinson's walking-stick or his design for

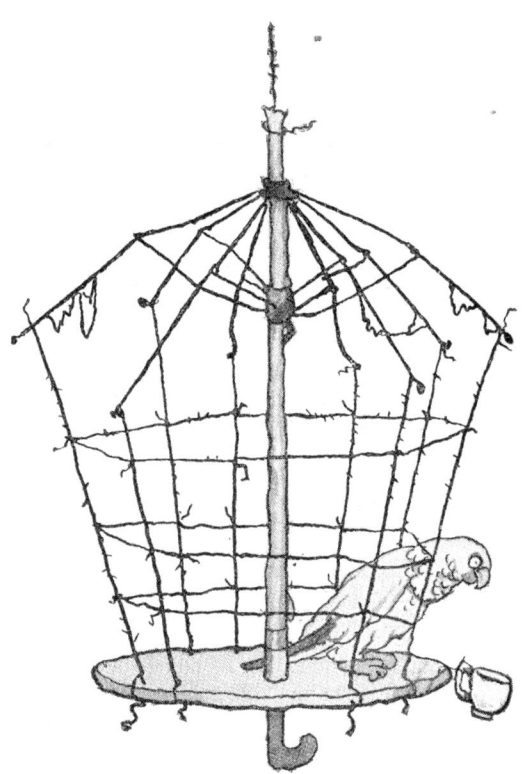

"*A* coverless umbrella converted into a decorative parrot's cage."

"*Old razor-blades, converted into dominoes, help to beguile the long winter evenings.*"

a modish toque. As he was the first to recognise, an electric bulb lends dignity to the cheapest cherry-wood, while as a hat ornament it is obviously cheaper than synthetic foliage and less irritating to humanitarians than a couple of stuffed seamews.

All that is ingenious enough; but I have yet to mention what I regard as this great man's crowning achievement. Alone and unaided, actuated by no lust for gain, but solely by a desire to help his fellow-men, he has solved a problem which has baffled the keenest brains in Europe. The problem—to beat about no more bushes—of What To Do With Old Razor-Blades.

Hitherto, I suspect, even such forceful personalities as Herr Hitler and Signor Mussolini have followed the common practice of letting their old razor-blades accumulate to the limit, thereafter detailing a myrmidon to pack them in bundles of ten and heave them privily into the Spree (or Tiber). That—substituting the Regent's Canal for the Tiber (or Spree)—is what *I* have always done, anyway.

No longer, however. Thanks to Mr. Heath Robinson, I know now that old razor-blades, converted into dominoes, will help to beguile the long winter evenings. (Nowadays, what with the high cost of forage and the tendency of Tax Collectors to bare their fangs if denied their lawful booty, no man discards his razor-blades until they are almost too blunt to dissect a hard-boiled egg; and consequently the risk of severed arteries and kindred ills is so small as to be negligible.)

Nor need they despair to whom dominoes do not appeal, for Mr. Heath Robinson has conclusively shown that attractive gewgaws—necklaces, ear-rings, book-markers, garden-shears and similar bric-à-brac—can be contrived by anybody having a little spare time and a lot of old razor-blades. It is even possible, with care and patience, to evolve a ravishing gown for the little woman from this unpromising material—a discovery which entitles the hero of this treatise to three rousing cheers from Britain's breadwinners and a prominent niche in Valhalla.

I have now said enough, I think, to show that in Mr. Heath Robinson the nation possesses an invaluable asset—particularly at a time like this, when Economy must be our watchword. One feels, indeed, that in a properly organised community he would be taken over by the State and classified with the Post Office and the B.B.C. as a Public Service. Who knows what that agile brain might not devise if it were sheltered from all mundane cares and allowed unlimited scope?

True, it seems to have devised nearly everything already; but I believe I am right in saying that it has yet to discover how to convert an ordinary moth-eaten old overdraft into a useful credit balance.

That, dear Mr. Heath Robinson, would be a triumph indeed!

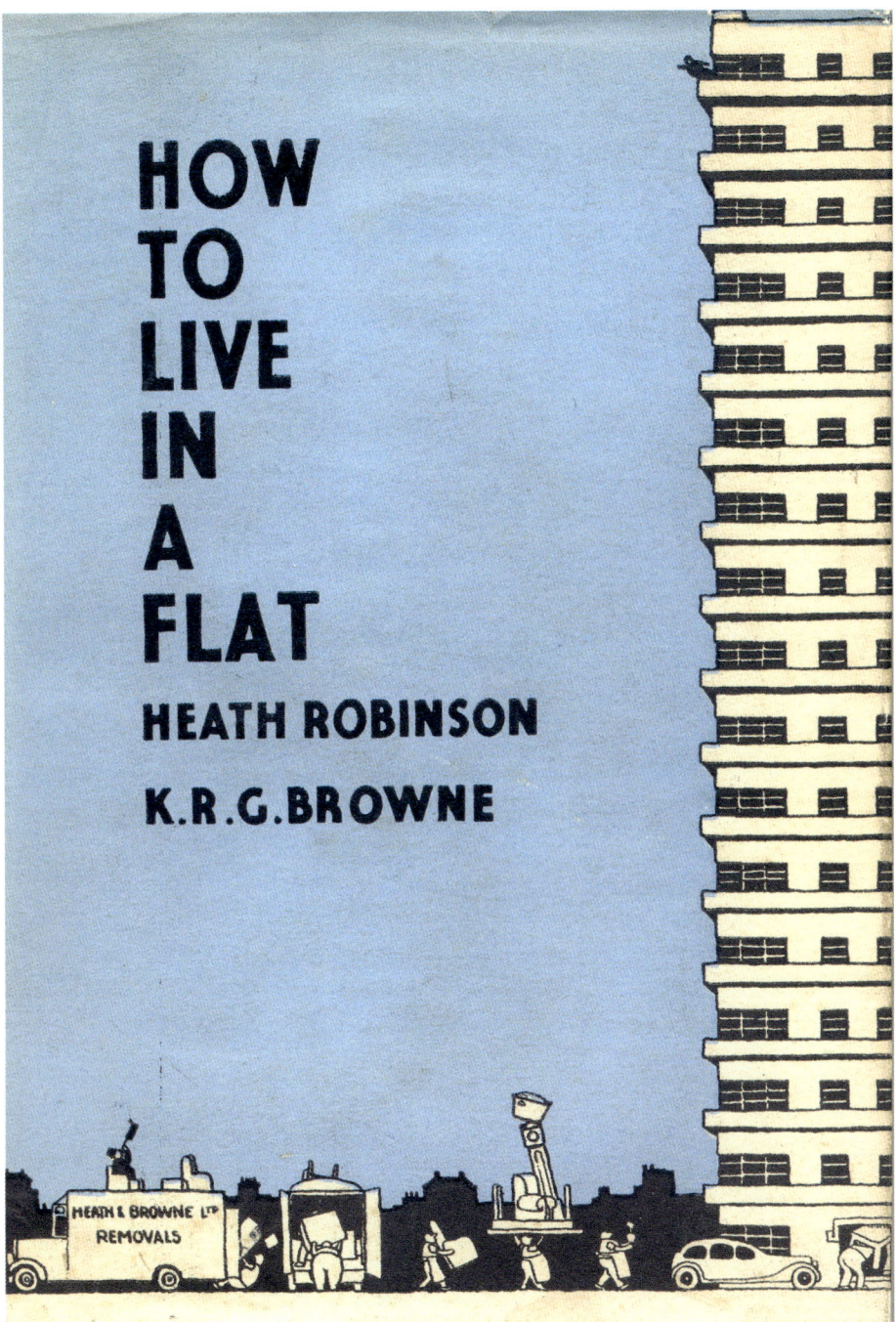

Dustwrapper design – How to Live in a Flat.

Heath Robinson's name had entered the language to describe a makeshift construction or a crazy contraption as early as 1912, but the series of books that perhaps did more than anything else to establish him in the public mind as "The Gadget King" was the "How to . . ." books. In 1935, Heath Robinson collaborated with a writer called KRG Browne to produce a small book called "How to Live in a Flat". As well as providing an opportunity for many of his contraptions, the book gave him an opportunity to satirise Modernism in architecture and design. Browne and Robinson produced three more books together in a similar vein before their partnership was brought to an untimely end by Browne's death in 1940. Following KRG Browne's death, Heath Robinson teamed up with a writer named Cecil Hunt, who was a neighbour in Highgate, to produce three more "How to . . ." books on wartime themes.

Modern carpet designs may provide endless entertainment.

The one-piece chromium steel dining suite.

Romantic possibilities of modern flats.

Roof hiking.

HOW TO LIVE IN A FLAT

A little mechanical help in rising gracefully from a lounge chair.

Handing up the Deoch an' Doris in a modern service flat.

HEATH ROBINSON CONTRAPTIONS

The Summer Cruise.

Out of practice at the beginning of the season.

When tea as well as sugar is rationed.

Doubling Gloucester cheeses by the Gruyere method

WORLD WAR II

Our Sixth Column frustrates a dastardly attempt by the fifth to tamper with a railway signal.

Stout members of the sixth column dislodge an enemy machine gun post on the dome of St Paul's.

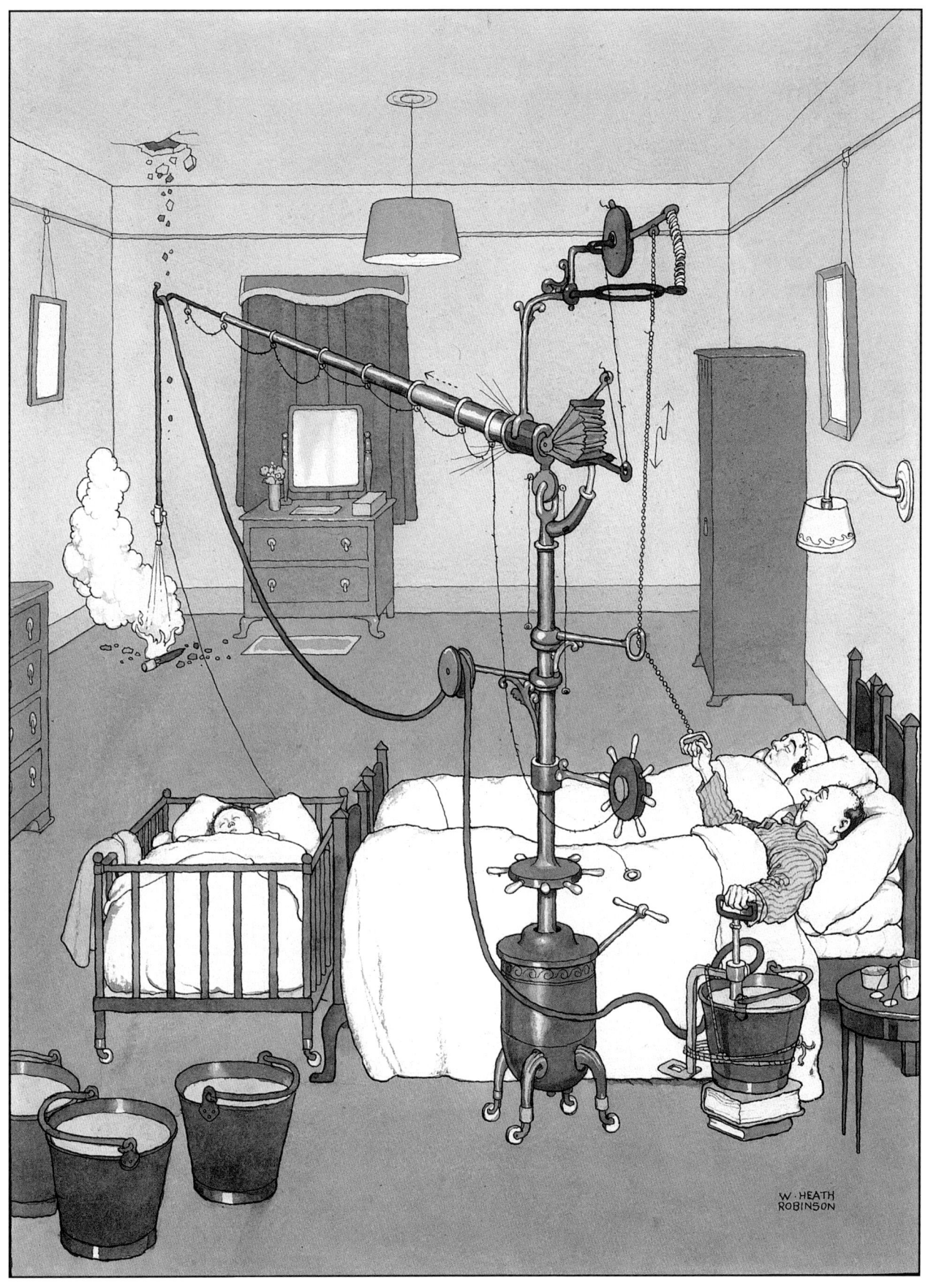

The ever-ready bedside bomb extinguisher.

Safe practice for paratroops.

Cooling buoys lowering the temperature of the Gulf Stream.

Is it true that physical pain is truly imaginary?

How do you put a square peg into a round hole?

Does dew rise or fall?

Do fish sleep?

How is the ship's anchor weighed?

Why are people disagreeable at breakfast time?

ACKNOWLEDGEMENTS

We are grateful to the following organisations that have provided images for this book.

The Cartoon Art Trust.
Pages 37, 43, 73, 95, 96.

Chris Beetles Limited.
Pages 36, 42, 48, 50-51, 53, 55, 63, 70, 103, 107, 115, 117, 119, 126, 129, 140, 145, 147, 157, 160, 165, 176, 179, 181, 183.

The Illustrated London News Picture Library.
Pages 9-34, 41, 44-47, 49, 52, 56-62, 64-69, 72, 74, 65-69, 72-74, 80, 82-83, 85-94, 97-102, 104-05, 109-14, 116, 120-21, 123-125, 127-28, 130-35, 138, 155-56, 158-59, 186-90.

The William Heath Robinson Trust.
Pages 35, 38-39, 71, 108, 141-2, 144, 146, 174-75, 178, 180, 182, 184-85, 191.

Other images from private collections.